I Spy the Rainbow

I Spy the Rainbow:

Becoming like a child

Fred Drummond

Authentic

First published 2004 by Authentic Media,
9 Holdom Avenue, Bletchley, Milton Keynes, MK1 1QR, UK
and PO Box 1047, Waynesboro, GA 30830-2047
www.authenticmedia.co.uk

British Library Cataloguing in Publication Data

A catalogue record for this book is available from
the British Library

ISBN 1-85078-565-1

Cover design by Phil Houghton
Print Management by Adare Carwin
Printed and Bound in Denmark by Nørhaven Paperback

Contents

Acknowledgements

I would like to thank my wife Caroline and sons Jonathan and Philip for their patience and encouragement. Thanks to June and Vanda for help on the manuscript. Thanks for the help and kindness of those at Authentic. Also thanks to my wider family and those of Perth Riverside who make it easier to see the rainbow.

Introduction

Rejoice in who you are

It is the most wonderful thing to know that God loves you. Not only that, but also that this God wants us to join with him in a journey of trust and fellowship. There can be nothing better than sharing our lives with the one who cares more for us than we care for ourselves.

Think for a moment. Isn't the Christian life the greatest honour and privilege that is available to any human being: to journey with God, and in journeying to be continually learning to know God better? Learning to love and be loved in ever deepening and more passionate ways. This is the calling of every disciple, in the good times and the not so good, in the celebration and the sacrifice, in the smiles and the sorrows. In all our experiences we share them with him who has had called us by name and has promised never to let us go.

Discipleship is not primarily about what we do but about whom we know. That was the experience of the first disciples. They were called to follow Jesus. They journeyed with him. They watched what he did and listened to what he said. Most of all they knew what it was to be loved by him, to enjoy his presence, to be with him.

The serving flowed from the knowing. It was the knowledge of his presence that made serving God possible.

Powerpoint – To be a disciple was not to follow a set of rules, it was to follow a person.

Growing closer to God should be the aim of all our lives. To live in that place of deepening closeness to God, as God takes us into an intimate place of belonging.

Many of us experience this throughout much of our Christian lives. Our spirituality is continually deepening, and we are moving forward in our journey with God. However, this is not the case all of the time. There are deserts as well as hilltops, depths as well as heights. This has been the case in my own life and maybe it has also been your experience too.

While visiting various churches, many share with me their struggles concerning the Christian life. These have been described in various ways. Some have talked about going through the motions; others have talked about lack of purpose and passion. A lack of enthusiasm and joy – everything seemed to be a bit of a struggle. While no one description dealt with all the expressions of unfulfilled spirituality, so the causes were equally varied. Fear, lack of encouragement, weight of expectation, failure to find a Christian community to be part of and busyness were all mentioned. All of these are robbing many people of the joy of their salvation and stunting their growth in dependency on the Lord.

As I write this I am sitting on Kinnoull Hill in Perthshire, Scotland. The trees, all different shapes and sizes, are bowing in the autumn breeze to their creator. The sky, blue – pale, deep, royal with polka dots of fluffy white in the distance. It is an amazing privilege to stop and wonder. The beauty of it all almost takes my breath away.

So often we appear to see things only in black and white, as if filters have been placed over our eyes allowing us only to see in dim shadow. It is so easy to lose sight of who God is and what he has done.

Powerpoint – Think of the wonder of nature its creator has made you.

How has this happened?

I believe that we have fallen into a subtle trap. We have thought that to be spiritual is to be in control. We feel that we have to grow up, be adult. To grow up and hold everything together is to be a mature sensible disciple.

However, it seems that our grown-upness has undermined our spiritual life. In holding things together we have let go of what is really important, and have been robbed of something wonderful and precious. We have lost the key to a growing relationship of love with God and have ignored the way of childlikeness. But it is as we become like little children that we discover a deepening and developing relationship with God. It is not in the holding on, but in the letting go that we find peace and power.

From time to time all of us live our spiritual lives as if in a fog. Clouds and mist swirl around our praying to and our following of Jesus. It can appear as though everything is dark and discouraging, without light and warmth. Life doesn't have to be like that. Just beyond the clouds is the rainbow. It is a symbol of covenant mercy and hope. To live remembering the rainbow is to reflect on the greatness of God and the wonder of his mercy. There are times when we all, with God's help, have to lift our eyes, hearts and spirits beyond the clouds and upwards to the wonder of our relationship with the God who has called us. This book is designed to help us all on our journey with God: walking through scriptural stories, ideas and reflections and asking God to draw us into a more intimate relationship with him. It is my prayer that this book will help us all to rejoice in our calling as God's people. It is an opportunity to move out of the clouds and spy the wonder of the rainbow.

1

What does it mean to be childlike?

What are the lessons we can learn from little children that have been lost to us?

I believe that they are rich and varied. In this book these lessons will be highlighted. I am convinced that if we take heed of them, we can be released into a deeper, more fulfilling relationship with God.

Many of us long for a renewed joy in our spirit, and a sense of value in our lives. Even the most spiritual of us have times of boredom, burden and wasted time. There are moments when we are lost in confusion and spiritual dryness, captive to doubt and fear, held in the damaging vice of fear, lack of encouragement and hopelessness. When we are faced with these things we try and stand as adults, using our strength and intellect to cope. However, sometimes these things can lead to great damage to our lives. Let me give you three examples.

The grey man

John is forty-three years old. He used to laugh a lot, but not much anymore. Things just seem so busy. Work, family, church: there was no time. How he just wants to relax and laugh with his children, but most of the time he shouts at them. They would be in bed now. Stuart was nine, he was full of fun – those freckles and that cheeky grin. Every day was an adventure. New games and imaginary friends – doctor, soldier and super-hero all rolled into one. John wondered why he had become so annoyed with Stuart, rather than enter his world and engage with him. He knew that his words had wounded his son, he could tell by the look in Stuart's eyes. Amy was his daughter, she was four and beautiful; she would be sleeping now, clutching Timmy, her multi-coloured teddy. She was growing so quickly. She looked like her mother.

A sudden stamping of feet brought John's mind back into the present. He was sitting in a damp room that felt cold. The meeting had been going for almost two hours, and like all the others it was so boring. He had tried everything to look interested. He had counted people, twenty-eight in all, listened to gossip, and smiled until his jaw felt sore – and all the time he felt like screaming, Why? It would be good to stand up right now and scream at the top of his voice. He wondered how folk would feel, what the response would be. John pictured Margaret, sitting in the row in front of him, her big body, red cheeks and bleached hair. He thought of her fainting with shock as he shouted, swooning and sway-ing, drawing a crowd around her and then managing to make a living out of the shock and sympathy.

John sat up and tried to focus. There appeared to be a cacophony of throat-clearing that always meant a deci-sion had been taken. If the Olympics were to include throat-clearing as an event, John was sure that St Luke's leadership was a certainty for gold.

When John had first been asked to join the leadership he felt so privileged. It was an honour, to serve God and lead the people forward. He had wondered how the meetings would go, to try and discern what the Spirit was saying. How the whole church would move forward. There were so many issues that needed looking at. It would be a big responsibility, but maybe he could make a difference.

Now two years on, he could hardly stand it. The meetings were mind numbingly dull. Hours were spent on money and maintenance issues. How could people talk for so long about the colour of the fences around the church? There didn't seem to be any sense of what God was doing in all this. Was it his fault, John wondered? Perhaps if he was more open and optimistic, maybe if he had exercised more faith, things might have been different. Maybe if his own spiritual life was more dynamic. Did he really care anymore?

At last the meeting ended. The pastor's prayer sounded like all his other prayers. John chatted to a few folk as he left, but made for the door as quickly as he could. He opened the thick wooden door and stepped out into the winter night. The rain blew into his eyes, mixing with his tears. This was ridiculous but everything seemed so heavy, so hard to deal with. Why can't I laugh? I used to be able to laugh. John started up the engine, put the car into gear and headed slowly down the side street. Why is my life so grey?

The fear factor

Marion sat at the long wooden table. Her hands propped up her chin as she stared into space. She pulled her pink thick dressing-gown tighter to her. It was cold. A sudden click invaded the silence as the blue plastic kettle in the corner reached boiling point. She got up from the chair, pushed her fair hair from her eyes and made herself some coffee. She felt weary. If only I could get a whole night of sleep, she thought. She had tried everything: reciting the Lord's Prayer, herbal tea, even a shot of whisky, but nothing worked. She could always get to sleep, that was never really the problem, but sleep, like many of her family and friends, soon departed. In the middle of the night she would wake, frightened, hot and confused. The picture was so clear to her. It seemed as if it was happening all over again, right in front of her eyes. She knew it was about to happen but she could do nothing to prevent it. For Marion every night was like watching a rerun of the same old video, but much worse.

The sun was shining and the air was warm. It had been a good start to the day. She had lunch with Anne. They went to the little Italian restaurant about ten minutes from the shopping centre. This was one of their favourite restaurants. They liked the clean white tablecloths and the small vase on each table, gently holding a single rose. It was so warm that they decided on a table outside. Marion had pasta, which was served with wonderful warm ciabatta bread, oozing with warm olive oil. Anne had a warm chicken salad. They dissected the office gossip, laughed and shared a bottle of Chianti. Feeling relaxed and confident, Marion headed for home. She came into her lounge. It was a bright and spacious room with a large couch, two easy chairs and a few bright prints of far away beaches on the walls. In the corner of the room sat a wooden unit on which was a large television. Marion dropped her bag on the floor and put her keys on the table. She slumped down onto the couch, kicked off her shoes and stretched out for the remote. The television flashed into life. At first Marion couldn't take it in, she thought it was a lunchtime film. The plane banked and headed straight for the buildings.

Marion held her breath, surely this couldn't be happening. The plane plunged like a dagger into a crumbled heart of metal and glass. Marion sat for a long time watching the murder and chaos unfold before her. It took her a long time before she cried, but when she did she thought she would never stop.

Marion's life has never been the same. Each night she sees the plane, she hears the screams of others and her own despairing shouts, and then she wakes in a sweat. She cries, and tears cascade down her cheeks soaking her pillow.

Sitting at the table she ponders her life. She doesn't go out much anymore. The world seems such an evil and empty horrible place. Everything frightens her and trust is very hard to give. Anne has phoned many times, but meals and laughter seem so trivial now, and Marion always finds a reason for not meeting. She used to go to church, she even sang in the choir. People said that she had a good voice. She didn't sing anymore; there was no point. Wherever she looked there was no hope.

Marion finished her coffee, put the empty cup beside the sink and switched off the light. As she made her way up the stairs to her bedroom she wondered why.

Giving up

She was draped in black from head to toe. She had red hair and deep purple lips and eyes. The nose-ring looked as though it must have been very painful to get done. There were numerous silver studs in her ears.

We met at a party. She drank vodka and Coke. We talked about music, art and films. Her name was Sarah. She asked me what I did in life. I told her that I was a church leader.

'Have you ever been to church?' I asked.

'Don't be stupid,' she laughed, 'it's for boring old people, my gran used to go. I don't need people telling me what to do.'

Sarah told me about her daughter Zoë. It was a strain trying to bring up a two-year-old by herself. Things were not easy but Sarah had managed to get a job in a pub. I invited them round to our house for a meal. They came.

It was a cold rainy day, typical for November. The usual crowd turned up, coming in through the dark doors hunched against the weather. It was a couple of minutes before the service was to begin. She stood there dripping, not sure where to go or what to do. Her small daughter held her hand. They went into a row at the back of the church. Zoë went into the crèche, someone spoke to them, and I gave a silent prayer of thanks.

It was a few weeks before we met again. Sarah talked about how uncomfortable she had felt. She had never been in a church before, but she had been going through a bad spell and thought that she would give it a try. It was too stuffy.

'I just couldn't follow it. It felt like people were looking at me all the time. I wondered if I had two heads, or if I had forgotten to put my top on. It was kind of weird. It's not really for people like me, is it?'

I tried to keep in touch. We met occasionally for coffee. Things were bad for Sarah. She was depressed, searching for some hope. I told her about the value that God placed upon her, and how special she was to him. She cried.

It was about two months later that I got a call. It was early in the morning. It was from Sarah's dad.

'Could you come to the hospital?' he pleaded.

I rushed along. Sarah had decided that the best thing she could do was die. She did.

It was a Tuesday evening, two days after Sarah's funeral. We gathered as a leadership team. Top of the agenda was how to raise funds to repair the roof. There was then a long debate on the merits of the 'terrible new hymns' that we sometimes sung. We looked at the reports from the church headquarters, yawned and said the benediction. We all got in our cars and went home. Angels wept, and wondered why.

Is this your life?

Perhaps you are able to identify with these stories more closely than you would like. Could it be that years of service have drained you of any real spiritual life and desire for God? Do you feel void, filled with fear or hopeless? Is the enthusiasm for life seeping from you like sweat from the pores of your soul?

He steps from the dressing room. He knows that he used to be really sharp. 'I used to have the fastest hands in the business,' he thinks to himself. I was a real contender. He remembered how the press had worshipped him and how he had been lied to by the hangers-on that called themselves his entourage. Twenty-three fights undefeated, and tipped to be the champ. His manager talked of chat shows and endorsements. Until the night when he came up against someone that bit faster, bit sharper. Suddenly no one wanted to know. The chance had gone. The glimpse of his dreams had teased him and moved on leaving him with only memories and old fight programmes.

He steps over the rope, into the ring. There isn't much noise, not a large crowd. Why should people pay to watch a failed contender? He weighs fifty pounds more than he did at his best. Seventy fights, he can't remember his record anymore and he doesn't care. Why does he still do it? It is the only way of life that he knows, and he doesn't know how to stop. He is chained to an empty way of life. He has given up on dreams now; he just tries to get by. The bell rings, he lifts his heavy frame up off the stool and prepares for more punishment.

Many of us have Christian lives that mirror the life of the broken boxer. We had dreams of what union with Christ would be like. Our first love flowed into active service and we were happy to give ourselves for the Kingdom. We had glimpses of what a loving relationship was; a life of joy peace and hope. Yet, the more that we served, the more the church asked us to do. The more we did, the more it was taken for granted that we would get the job done. Our lives became filled with meetings and committees, debate and decisions.

There are many reasons why this can happen to all of us. The joy of relationship can get lost in the control that we put on life and the pace at which we live. Between work, church, the pace of life, and lack of fellowship, the spiritual oasis of our lives dries up. Jesus is someone we work for, not someone we journey with anymore. Rather than being part of a community we feel like individuals cast adrift in a sea of fear and disappointment. We carry on because we don't know how to break free. We plod on, steady, dependable and joyless. We do everything in a well thought out and planned way. We are mature and adult about life, church and faith. Perhaps that is our problem. The life that we are living is not what God would have for us. God does not want us to live as defeated, spiritually punch-drunk Christians.

In Jesus' famous image of the 'Good Shepherd' he contrasts the work of the thief, who comes only to steal and destroy, with his own work: 'I have come that they may have life, and have it to the full' (Jn. 10:10). Don Carson commenting upon this verse in John writes: 'Within the metaphorical world, life...to the full suggests fat, contented, flourishing sheep, not terrorised by brigands; outside the metaphorical world it means that the life Jesus' true disciples enjoy is not to be construed as more time to fill (merely everlasting life) but life at its scarcely imagined best, life to be lived.'[1]

Jesus came to bring us life in all its fullness. That is a growing deepening journey where we grow ever closer to the Lord who loves us. While faith does not exclude us from the hurts and sorrows of the world, it does grant us resources beyond ourselves to cope with being in the world. To journey along with Jesus is to go the way of the cross, with all that that entails. However, it is also to live in the grace of God, acknowledging God's undeserving goodness in our lives. Living in this goodness should open up for us a new life. A life of hope and joy created so that we may flourish and prosper. A life where we rejoice in who we have become in Christ. Growing in delight at his presence and making a difference in the world.

In *The Message*, Eugene Peterson translates the same verse in John 10 as a 'more and better life than we ever dreamed of.'[2] How have we drifted so far from this possibility of the life of freedom and grace? Perhaps, if we look at this incident in the gospels and listen to Jesus' words afresh we will be able to move on in our Christian lives.

Powerpoint – Jesus wants us to experience life in abundance, not life in constant defeat.

Reflection

Question – Are there particular things that hinder your spiritual life?

Action – Make a list of these things and reflect upon them. Picture Jesus looking at the list with you. Think of his gaze of love and his healing touch. What would his response be to the things that you have shared?

Prayer

Lord, you are gracious and caring. Thank you for loving me and for your commitment to me. Help me to so open my life to you that I grow in my journey of faith. As I read this book, use the things that are relevant to me to draw me closer to you.

In Jesus' name.

Amen.

---

1   Don Carson, *The Gospel According to John*, (Downers Grove: IVP, 1991) p. 385

2   Eugene Peterson, *The Message*, (Colorado Springs: NavPress, 1993) p. 248

2

Jesus and childlikeness

Got to get closer

The sun had risen and the day was warm. The air felt very heavy and I stifled a yawn. I rubbed the sleep from my eyes. It seemed a long time since I had had a good night's sleep. Not that I would ever complain – it is a privilege to share two children with my husband. They were both sleeping now and the house was quiet. I was really glad about that, as there was a lot to do that morning. I was not sure about what would happen that day, but David, my husband was really excited about it. When he talked his blue eyes shone and sparkled and his hands waved around. I'd never seen him so excited. He has the dreams and I do the work. Such is the lot of the wife and mother.

So there I was with my list of things to do. First, I had to get the food together. I take some barley loaves and some wheat bread. As we could be away for a while, I decide to take some lentils and beans. I love their smell and they taste really great. I also get some of the milk that came fresh from the cows that morning. Lastly some grapes to eat with the bread. It seems a lot, but I know that it would all be eaten. David likes his food.

Having taken time to prepare the food I then get the children ready. I go to our son and shake him gently by the shoulder. He is a sound sleeper. Very slowly he begins to move. 'Elkanah, it's time to get up. Time to move, sleepy head.'

He lifts his small hand to his eyes and gently rubs away the signs of a good night's sleep. I stop and gaze at him. He is tall for his age, with thick black hair and deep bright eyes like his father's. Four years old. We are so proud God blessed us with a strong, healthy boy. I turn to get the baby ready to go. Her name is Jemima (meaning dove), for she has brought great contentment to us, although in the middle of the night that peace is sometimes in short supply. David says that she looks like me.

'Rachel,' he says, 'she has your smile and your habit of getting your own way by touching my heart.'

David has been different lately. Ever since he heard the teacher. I remember so clearly his excitement when he returned. He had heard of this new rabbi and wanted to hear him for himself. I had laughed.

'Not another new teacher?' I mocked.

However, that night David came back a different man. I could tell as soon as he burst through the door.

'Sit down Rachel, I have to tell you all about the day,' he said.

He could hardly stop talking, words poured from his mouth. The crowd had been huge and the teacher had been near the top of the hill with his closest disciples. The rabbi started to talk to the crowd.

'I can still remember the words that he said:

Blessed are the poor in spirit, for theirs is the kingdom of heaven.

Blessed are they who mourn for they shall be comforted.
Blessed are the meek for they shall inherit the earth.
Blessed are those who hunger and thirst for righteousness,
for they will be filled.
Blessed are the merciful, for they will be shown mercy.
Blessed are the pure in heart, for they will see God.
Blessed are the peacemakers, for they shall be called sons of
God.
Blessed are those who are persecuted because of righteous-
ness, for theirs is the kingdom of heaven.[1]

'It was not just the words he said but the way he said them
Rachel. He had such, such authority. When he spoke I
thought that he was speaking only to me. I ran part of the
way home. I don't know why but I want to laugh.'

Then he had hugged me.

David had come home to tell me that the teacher was
in the area again and we were all going to hear him.

'What about the children?' I asked.

'We will take them with us.'

'To hear a preacher?' I looked at him sceptically.

'Let's take food, we can listen together.' He looked at
me with tears in his eyes. 'You and the children are my
gifts from God, and I want you all to see the teacher – he
comes from God.'

That's the reason that morning was busy. I didn't
know what to expect, I felt excited and a little frightened. I wondered what that day might bring.

'Are we ready to go?' David asked, as he came
through the door.

'Almost,' I reply, 'I just have to change your darling
daughter first.'

'Ah' he smiled, 'I will just check the animals.' He beat
a hasty retreat.

Soon we were ready for the journey.

The blessing

There was a large crowd. The first thing we noticed was the mix of people. There were young and old, rich and poor, Pharisees and academics. I was shocked to see some who I never thought would come and listen to a preacher. With a bit of determination, and the use of my young-mother-under-pressure look, we managed to get a good view and settled down.

As Jesus began to speak, what he said seemed to touch every heart and challenge every mind. He told a story about two people praying. God was interested in our prayers when they came from the heart. Then he said some words about the need for people to stay humble before God. I was captivated by the way he looked. His eyes shone with a real passion, and yet as he looked at the people crowded around him, he appeared to be deeply moved. There were many people trying to get close to him, the sick and diseased. They believed that he could make a difference to them. So did I. He was no ordinary man, he was sent from God.

David nudged me. I turned to look at him. His eyes were moist and tears were trailing down his face, cutting lines through the dust. It was the first time I had seen my husband cry since the birth of our son.

'I want him to bless our children,' he said, 'I want him to touch our babies. They are our gift from God and he comes from God. I must get the children to him.'

I put my hand in his and he squeezed it. With my children beside me, and holding on to David's hand I felt a great sense of peace, even in the midst of the crowd. It was a special moment. I immediately knew that David was right. I passed Jemima to David, and then took Elkanah by the hand and we started to ease our way through the people in front of us.

It was as we approached the front of the crowd that two of his followers came to us. David told me later that they had been fishermen before.

'What do you want with the master?' the taller one asked.

David explained that we wanted the teacher to bless our children. The tall one shook his head.

'Can't you see that the master is busy, and he is tired? There are so many people and they all want something from him. If you want a baby blessed take him to a priest. He doesn't have the time.'

'Please,' said David, 'it would be a great blessing on all our family. It is clear that this man is from God.'

Before the men could speak again, Elkanah squirmed from my grasp and pushed out of the crowd near to Jesus. One of his followers laid a hand on him to prevent Elkanah from getting too close. At that moment Jesus looked over at us. In a clear voice of authority he told his followers, 'Let the little children come to me, do not hinder them, for the Kingdom of God belongs to such as these.'[2]

At these words the followers let us through. I lifted up Jemima to him and he blessed her. Then he bent down towards Elkanah, took his hand and looked around at the crowd. They had all gone very quiet, wondering what was going to happen next. He raised himself up, still holding on to our son's hand.

'I tell you the truth, anyone who will not receive the Kingdom of God like a little child will never enter it.'

In a way it seemed as if we were not important and that Jesus' full attention had been on our children. Yet in another way it felt like he was speaking directly to us. What did he mean we had to become like little children? I was about to ask him when a rich young ruler asked about inheriting eternal life. Elkanah was back at my side, the chance to ask was gone.

As we travelled back to our home we hardly spoke. Something wonderful had happened to us, and it held our entire feelings captive. It was as if speaking was unimportant. It could add nothing and might even rob us of something. Yet many times since that day we have talked. We have marvelled at his words and compassion on people like us. From that time we have praised God and never doubted God's love for us.

As my children lie sleeping they are secure, warm and loved, and as they gently snore I still ponder what it means to become like a little child.

Thinking it through

Perhaps it didn't happen quite like that. However, according to the Gospel of Luke we can be sure that Jesus does make time to bless babies. Jesus says, 'I tell you the truth, anyone who will not receive the kingdom of God like a little child will never enter it' (Lk. 18:17).

For several years I thought that these words meant that eagerness and openness were the qualities required to enter the Kingdom. Several commentators have suggested that it is the sincerity and eagerness characteristic of children that makes them fitting examples of what those hoping to enter the Kingdom of God should be like. By nature adults are a complete contrast to this. Adults seek to be grown ups. To be a grown up is to be self-assured, independent, secure and having things all worked out. All of these characteristics hinder people from entering the Kingdom of God.

While I accept this line of thinking, I wonder whether it goes nearly far enough. If Jesus only wanted an image to contrast with the proud and self-assured, there were lots of people that Jesus met who would have been clearer illustrations. Women, lepers or tax collectors are all examples of those on the margins of society who are no longer self-assured, independent and proud. Could it be that the characteristics of a child might have a lot more to say to us than we had thought? Perhaps by looking at these characteristics we might find areas of spiritual truth that would lead us into the type of kingdom living that marks the life of a faithful and growing disciple.

Powerpoint – We can grow in our spiritual life if we learn from little children.

Love the unlovely

Before we do, let me underline one point.

It was just into the early evening. It was a wet cold winter's night in Scotland. I drove up from Hay Street onto Ainslie Gardens and then turned right onto Ainslie Place. My headlights shone on his face. He looked to be about eight-years-old. There appeared to be two channels of green lava running from the volcano in the middle of his face. He seemed to be using his sleeve as an attempt to stem the flood. It wasn't working. He was sitting in the middle of the road in his imaginary Ferrari. Actually it was a rusted supermarket trolley with green wheels. One of his friends was pushing him. I don't know if he was winning at Daytona or Brands Hatch but his race was rudely interrupted.

He was not very impressed by my interruption. I had to stop. He didn't move. I tried to wave and ask him to move. He waved back in a very unflattering way with only one finger. I peeped the horn and slowly and antagonistically he moved the sports trolley to the side of the road. I looked at him and wondered why he was out at that time of night on a wet and cold evening. I felt sad. Did nobody really care? Then I remembered a Saviour who welcomed children. Dirty hands, scowling faces, cheeky grins and everything else. I sat in the car and started to laugh. What would Jesus have made of this child in a rusty shopping trolley? I knew that he would love him. It is so important that we remember how loved we are by God. There are lots of things in the world that make us feel ordinary, just one in a crowd. We are never just one in a crowd to God. His grace is unique.

It doesn't matter how far we wander, how dirty we appear nor how small our dreams have become. God never loses his interest in us.

Powerpoint – No matter how weak and broken we feel God never stops caring for us.

Reflection

1. Reflect upon God's love for you. How does it affect your day-to-day living?
2. If Jesus loves the unlovely then how might that affect our view of others?

Meditation

A thousand stars shine in the deep dark skies.
He knows each one.
A thousand grains of sand lies silently as a beach.
He knows each one.
A thousand leaves lie as a golden carpet.
He knows each one.
You are never just one in a crowd with God.

Prayer

Lord, thank you for calling me by name.
Help me to relax and allow you to change me.
In Jesus' name.
Amen.

---

[1] Matthew 5: 2-10
[2] Luke 18: 15-17

3

Trust

Jump right in

It is summer time and school is closed for the holidays. As a dad with two children I take on the role of full time chauffeur during holiday times. Earlier in the day the boys had been dropped off at the leisure centre and it was my job to pick them up. The swimming pool is always very busy.

I am a little early so I order a coffee and find a table overlooking the pool. The pool is full of plastic palm trees and water slides. Children queue up to get a turn on the largest slide. There is a lot of laughter and a real buzz about the place. Everyone seems to be having a great time. I settle down to read the local paper to catch up on news.

After a little while I scan the pool for my children. As I look around I see an adult smiling, eyes bright and arms stretched out. At the side of the pool is a small child. He has sandy coloured hair and his face is covered in freckles. He has a large bright inflatable ring around his middle. He looks at his father and then a huge grin spreads across his face. The boy then jumps straight into the water and into the parent's arms. There is a clear bond of trust between the man and the boy. Swimming alongside the man comes a woman who I took to be part of the family, maybe the mum. She stands a little bit away and urges the boy to swim to her. He looks at her and shakes his head. She smiles and urges him to try. With determination he leaves the father's arms and heads off towards the mum. It is only a few strokes, and they wouldn't win any marks for style. A cross between a doggy paddle and a hippopotamus in mud. Yet to look at father, mother and child you would have thought that a gold medal had been won.

There was a clear trusting, a deep bond between parent and child. The child trusts the parent and grows through that bond. I could see the closeness, and it was providing a source of motivation and encouragement for the child and a source of joy for the parents. When the child took that step back at the edge of the pool and then came forward to jump, he did so believing that his dad was going to be there to catch him. What if the dad turns his back or gets distracted and puts his hands down? The child doesn't think of these things. The child is secure enough to jump because he believes he will be caught. The parent will be there – the one who called him to take the leap is the one who will catch him. That trust is what helps the child grow and develop his confidence. It is this environment of trust that makes it possible to jump. Taking the leap is only possible through the bond of trust.

To be childlike is to find a trusting bond with the parent, which leads us to growth and motivation. It is to have an open heart that allows us to step out of our own place into the unknown because we trust the one who calls us. This is the place of trust that we are called into if we are to be God's people.

People that jumped right in

At the beginning of Genesis 12 we find Abraham (still
called Abram at this point). He is living in Haran. He is
there with his family because some years earlier God
had called him to leave his country and people and go to
the land that God would show him. He leaves and set-
tles into a new home with his family.[1] After the death of
his father Terah, Abraham gets another call from God.
Perhaps it is underlining the original call, or maybe a
second stage on the journey. Whichever it was, it was a
clear call from the Lord on the life of Abraham.

> 'Leave your country, your people and your father's house-
> hold and go to the land I will show you.
> I will make you a great nation and I will bless you;
> I will make your name great, and you will be a blessing.
> I will bless those who bless you, and whoever curses you I
> will curse;
> and all peoples of the earth,
> will be blessed by you.' (Gen. 12:1-5)

God was going to do amazing things through Abraham.
Look at the promises that God makes to him. Of course
Abraham is not told how difficult it is going to be. Nobody
hands him a road map pointing out all the pitfalls and
dangers. There is no itinerary of what to expect on the
journey. All Abraham has are these great promises. He has
to make a decision of whether to stay in the safety or step
out in faith. He has to decide whether to become like a little child and jump at his father's calling, or to stay on the
edge of the pool. It could not have been an easy decision
to make.

Derek Kidner in his commentary on Genesis makes
this point when he writes: 'Abram must exchange the

known for the unknown, and find his reward in what he could not live to see (a great nation), in what was intangible (thy name) and in what he would impart (blessing).[2] To exchange the known for the unknown because God had asked him to. The motivation comes from the bond with the person who calls. Does he have trust in the one who asks him to leave behind the past and step into the future? We have no indication of whether it was a difficult decision. No idea if Abraham had any doubts or fears. I think that as we read this part of Abraham's story we are expected to marvel at his conviction and determination. Verse 4 simply says, 'So Abraham left.'

Is that not amazing? He simply left. He had the trust to accept the call and move forward. He trusted enough to come off the ledge, and step into the air of unpredictability, knowing that his loving Father would catch him. The one who called him would not fail him.

Powerpoint – The motivation to exchange the known for the unknown comes from the relationship we have with the one who calls.

Making a meal of things

The call to step out and follow that we witnessed in Abraham's life has a close parallel in the call of the disciples by Jesus. I like to dwell on the story of the tax-collector Levi found in the Gospels of Matthew, Mark and Luke.[3] Having already called three Galilean fishermen, Jesus now turns his attention to a tax collector. If Levi had spent much time talking about that life-changing day I wonder what he might have said.

* * *

It is not easy to be branded a traitor. To be looked down on because of your job. I used to see hatred in people's eyes – if they looked at me at all. I knew that things would be difficult when I became a tax collector, but to live with the hatred all the time was slowly killing me. No matter what they all say about us not caring, it's not true. We all want respect. They called me collaborator and cheat. Was it my fault that the taxes were so high? I didn't set them. People had to pay ground tax, income tax and poll tax. That was the law. People criticised because we worked with pagans and touched Gentile coins, but that was just part of the job.

There were perks of course. The money was good and I had friends in the same type of work, but it didn't make up for the longing to be accepted, to have some meaning and purpose for life. I often pondered these things as I sat in the tax booth, collecting and counting. I was thinking about these things on that day. It was hot and we were busy. There had been many ships docking and that meant more money. Then I saw the group coming up the road. They were still a good distance from me but I could make out that the one at the centre was talking, and the others seemed to be listening intently.

There was something about them that made me continue to watch. As they approached I realized that I had seen them before. It was the teacher and healer who was making a bit of a name for himself. People said that he spoke with real power and that he was a man of God. I was a bit sceptical. I have seen and heard lots of stories during the time that I've worked in this booth. Travelling preachers with their disciples are always coming this way. All with some miracle to share with us. Some say that this one was different, this Jesus.

As they came almost level with the booth they stopped. Jesus looked at me. It was a look that I can't

describe. It seemed to penetrate my heart and very soul.
I had to look away. I didn't know what to say. For some
reason I felt like crying. Me, a hardened tax collector,
crying. No one would believe it. Imagine if some of my
friends were here – how they would have laughed.
Tough, strong, cynical Levi touched by a look. 'You've
been in the sun too long my friend,' they would have
said. 'Maybe you need a holiday.' Yet, if they had seen
that look, I think they would have been silent, just as I
was.

In those few seconds of silence all of these thoughts
whirled around my mind. Finally I had the courage to
lift my eyes back to his. Then he spoke to me.

'Follow me,' was all he said.

It was enough. I didn't have to think or ponder. As
soon as he asked me to join him I knew it was the right
thing for me to do. It would mean a whole new
lifestyle. To walk out on this job was a huge step. I
would be leaving everything behind. Any chance of
wealth, any position would all be gone if I left the tax
booth and followed. Yet I was aware that suddenly a
meaning of hope had entered my life. It was not so
much the words as the way he said them. I left everything and followed him.

Just to have left and followed seemed such a wonderful freedom. If you had asked me where it would all end
up, I would not have been able to tell you. I didn't even
know where we would end up that day. All I had been
asked was to follow and I did. Maybe if I had taken
more time to think about it I would have been more
scared. No I don't think I would. Once I had heard Jesus
talk to me I knew that I had to follow him.

Then I began to think. If Jesus could change me so
quickly, then I had to let my friends have the chance of
meeting him and hearing these things for themselves. I

decided to hold a banquet and invite the people that I had met through my work, and others that I had got to know. I also wanted to honour Jesus. He was the one who had changed my life and I wanted, in a small way, to show him how I felt. Maybe my friends would think that I had finally flipped altogether, but I didn't care. This was a chance for them. I was not sure how things would go. In fact I did not know how Jesus would respond. After all he was a teacher, a prophet, one sent from God. My friends were tax collectors and sinners. Would Jesus really want to spend time with them? To eat with them would be a big thing: making friends with people like us would be a social disgrace. I knew that he had called me, so maybe he was showing that God had a place for people like us.

He came and he ate and he identified with us all. His presence caused a bit of controversy, but some of us will never forget the words he said to those who criticised him.

'It's not the healthy who need a doctor but the sick,' Jesus answered them, 'I have not come to call the righteous but sinners to repentance.'

Levi was a guy who had the chance to step out. Literally from out of his tax booth, but much more importantly to step out of the life he had into a life that would unfold one step at a time. All he had to go on was the fact that he had been called, and that it was Jesus who called him. His response is immediate and wonderful. Not only does he follow right away but he also left everything behind. Not only did he jump into the pool, he doesn't even look back to the edge. In fact, Levi starts attempting a few strokes right away. Having a banquet for Jesus, inviting your old friends. That was really moving on towards the deep end. What would the friends say? This was a public declaration that Jesus was now central to who Levi was.

Powerpoint – Following Jesus can't be done in secret.

How was it possible for Levi to take such a life-changing step? It was only possible through having that childlike trust. Levi was able to step out because it was Jesus who had asked him to take that leap. Jesus was the person whom Levi believed could be trusted. Confidence is the biggest key to trusting. If we are confident in the person who calls us to follow, we don't need a road map that points out every turn on the road. Levi was not given extra information. He was not aware of the joys and the hardships that would shape his life over the next few years. He wasn't given these things because he didn't need them. All he required was the voice of Jesus calling to him to follow. To follow into the unknown, that is trust.

Powerpoint – If we are confident in the person who calls us to follow we don't need a road map.

Taking the plunge

Many of us know the joy of giving our lives over to Jesus Christ. We have joined the world-wide community of faith, trusting in the greatness and goodness of God. We found new life in the finished work of Jesus. A life that was to be full and have a different quality than we had experienced before. Yet many of us find it difficult to live the life of trust. After that initial commitment we seem to fall back into what we think is the safety of understanding.

Powerpoint – It is easy to head for safety.

If we were at the edge of the pool we would want some
answers before we left the edge.

What's under the surface?

Is he really able to catch me?

What will happen if I don't get caught?

What will everybody say if I was just to jump?

Our minds would be filled with a mass of questions.
We would find a million reasons for not stepping off the
ledge. We would feel more content watching others
jump rather than jump ourselves. In this fear we lose the
chance to grow in our relationship with God and we lose
the motivation to move forward into the joy of sharing
the journey into the unknown with God.

Perhaps there are many reasons why many of us find
stepping out in trust so difficult. One of the main reasons is
that our trust has often been abused. In our relationships we
have encountered let down and severe disappointment. We
have become vulnerable in sharing who we are with others
only to have that abused.

I have spoken to many Christians who have felt hurt
and discouraged by other people's responses to them.
The net effect of these rejections is that we now don't
trust people very easily. If we keep people at arm's
length then we can't be hurt. Instead of remaining open
to people we weigh things up noting the pluses and
minuses of every situation. When this attitude marks
our spiritual life we find it hard to follow Jesus.

How sad this is when our lives are marked by a lack
of trust. Just as sad as when this is the main characteristic of our churches. Are our leadership meetings
marked by statements of trust? Are we growing closer
as a team to God? Rather than heeding the call and
jumping into the pool, many of our churches would
commission a report on the financial implications of the
jump. Then we would set up a sub-group to find out

details concerning the temperature of the water. In trying to be adult we sometimes close off the possibilities of following the call.

Powerpoint – We can all find justifiable reasons for not stepping out.

A child does not think like this, rather the child would look at who was calling them. It is the bond of trust that matters, and every step of trust leads to the motivation to another step and then another. In order for us to be the type of people that God wants us to be, to live in the sort of way that God calls us to live, we have to come to a place like a little child that trusts God. We must have the bond of faith in the God who loves us and gave himself for us. That trust that is able to say to God, 'Lord I believe your arms are held out to catch me. I don't need all the answers, and I don't need to have my life all worked out for me. All I need to know is that you will catch me.' A response that is childlike is a response of intimacy. It is a step of bonding and motivation.

Powerpoint – Many of us miss huge possibilities of growth through lack of trust.

Many of us shy away from this huge opportunity. When we do refuse, we fail to discover the joy of moving on with God. To trust without questioning, without weighing up all options. Is Jesus indicating that it is in this trusting that we begin to experience kingdom living? Rather than seeking absolutes, trusting should be enough for us. Too often we require a written contract in triplicate, when God calls us to jump in.

Lesslie Newbigin was a man of great insight and understanding about mission and the Christian life. He wrote several very helpful books. In *Proper Confidence* he writes these words: 'The proper confidence to a Christian is not the confidence of one who claims possession of demonstrable and indubitable knowledge. It is the confidence of one who has heard and answered the call that comes from God through whom and for whom all things were made; follow me.'[4]

This is to move at the call of the one who calls us by name. To live with a faith that simply follows. To trust like a little child.

Powerpoint – Too often we require a written contract in triplicate when God calls us to jump right in.

Reflection

Think of the words taken from the hymn by John Sammis.[5]

Not a shadow can rise, not a cloud in the skies,
But His smile quickly drives it away;
Not a doubt nor a fear, not a sigh nor a tear,
Can abide while we trust and obey.

Refrain
Trust and obey, for there is no other way
To be happy in Jesus, but to trust and obey.

What does it mean to trust and obey?

Action

Try talking to someone new at church. Reach out to someone and see how God works through this small step.

Go somewhere different, perhaps for a coffee. Give yourself space to listen for God.

Prayer

Lord, thank you that you call me to the adventure of faith.
Help me to daily trust you,
Help me to follow where you lead
that I may grow in my journey with you.
Through Jesus, my Saviour and friend.
Amen.

[1] See Stephen's speech in Acts 7
[2] Derek Kidner, *Genesis*, (Leicester: IVP, 1967) p. 114
[3] See Matthew 9: 9-13; Mark 2: 13-17; Luke 5: 17-22
[4] Lesslie Newbigin, *Proper Confidence*, (Grand Rapids: Eerdmans, 1995) p. 105
[5] Verse 2 and the chorus taken from 'Trust and Obey' by John Sammis

4

Imagination

Open your eyes

The noise was coming from a room at the front of the house. I quietly pushed open the door and peeked inside. The room had a deep green carpet and had several chairs scattered around. In the centre of the room there was a coffee table. I scanned the room but at first I could not identify where the sound was coming from. In the corner of the room there was a green couch and I realized that the sounds were coming from there.

'Fall back men,' shouted the faceless voice, 'we are under attack.'

Suddenly came the sound of attack. Rrrrrrrrrrrr...ta ta ta ta boom boom.

'Under cover men!'

It was clear that the young voices were getting more and more excited about the battle that was taking place to declare ownership on the corner of my front room. I stretched up on my toes to get a better look. The two young boys were engrossed in the battle and didn't even realize that I was there. I watched for a few minutes, as they inhabited this thrilling other world. Toy soldiers

were scattered around the floor, some trying desperately
to find some cover from the low-flying fighter plane that
was making the noisy attack as it swooped down in this
little boy's hand.

I went back through to the kitchen to get the little
commanders a snack. Once I had made the juice and put
out the biscuits I took the tray through to the theatre of
battle. I approached the door just as a triumphant shout
went up. Goal! To my surprise the battle zone had
become a sports pitch and the warriors were now foot-
ballers desperate to lead their teams to victory. The floor
still looked like a battlefield to me, with things scattered
all around, but in another corner the World Cup final
was now being played. However, just at a vital moment,
the pitch was invaded by a snack-wielding adult.

To play is a vital part of a child's life. To use imagination and to create new worlds helps children develop. If
they are to grow mentally, physically and socially then
play is essential. Play is the environment of the imagination; of unseen worlds and untold riches, of hidden
possibilities and vast adventures.

I wonder if you have seen the film *Pete's Dragon*. I
have watched it a lot over the years. It is a great family film. There are good guys and villains as well as
some comedy characters and good songs. The central
character is the young boy Pete and a loveable dragon
called Eliot. The film begins with Pete travelling on the
back of, and talking to the invisible dragon. The young
boy has had an almost Cinderella-like life. He works
for a family of shady characters. As the story unfolds
we discover that Pete has no home and does not know
who or where his parents are. In fact he had been sold
to the family. One of the famous songs in the movie
tells us that the family has a bill of sale for Pete and he
belongs to them. They regard him as property to be

bought and sold. He is thought of by the family as an object to be used and discarded.

Pete and the dragon head to Passamaquoddy, a small coastal town, in the hope of friendship and a new start. These are precisely what they find scattered amongst a few adventures they have along the way. Most of the comedy comes from the fact that there are times when only Pete can see the dragon. Fences fall apart, animals are frightened and footprints are found in new cement. Everyone can see the effects but no one can see why these things are happening. The only one who knows is the young boy and the playful invisible dragon.

For the boy, his experience of life as it was had been hard and unloving. His only real friend was Elliot the dragon. It is in the alternative life with Elliot that he glimpses what life could be. He sums this up in a song that he sings with his new friend who is called Nora. He tries to explain to Nora about his friend Elliot the dragon. In Elliot Pete has found a true friend one with whom to share dreams and cares. Pete thinks that it is important to spend time on a friendship like that because they are not easy to find. The friendship needs to be fanned and developed to make sure that it grows. It is the opportunity to glimpse that other world of friendship and understanding that enables Pete not only to cope but also to overcome.

Spiritually, I believe that it is the same for us. Many of us are stuck in a spiritual rut. We thing that there should be something deeper or more life enhancing than we have experienced, but we don't know where to look. Our Christian lives are marked by dedication, commitment and faithfulness, and we work hard at these characteristics of discipleship. All of these things are good and important marks of the disciple. Yet we miss out on hope, peace and worth. We get so caught up in the pressures and demands of the culture in which we live and work, that we lose sight of the alternative life of the Kingdom of God. In order to grow and develop as spiritual people we must be prepared to step out of the narrow world-view that we have and glimpse the alternative that is found in God. There is more taking place that we can see. God calls us to reflect upon and widen our vision, taking us into new possibilities. Many of us are wary of things like reflection and imagination. We like to work in straight lines and with control.

I can only imagine

The Oxford Dictionary defines imagination as 'the mental faculty forming images or concepts of external objects not present to the senses' and ' the ability of the mind to be creative or resourceful.' So imagination involves taking the time to be creative and enter into the unknown. It is taking the time to discern 'what might be' rather than always living in the 'what is'.

Our belief in God should fire our imagination because God is a creative God. Stop and consider the wonder of the created order. Take a minute just to stop and look around you. Oh I know that you are busy but it will be worth it. Gaze at the shades of blue in the sky. Try and count them. Notice the subtle differences of tone and shade. Our world is a glorious place if we just stop and consider it. If we believe that God has had his fingerprint on all created order then God is the master creator, displaying an array of creative energy and diversity that is far beyond our imagination.

One of the problems we face is that life is so busy that we are blinded to the beauty of the things right in front of us. We don't have time to ponder other worlds because we are rushing around this one. I hear you say, 'All this imagining and other world stuff is just for dreamers. I've got things to achieve that have to be done now.' That may be our attitude but is it God's? As we read the Bible are we not being continually invited into a shared journey of the imagination? Does God not call us to see, not just to see with our eyes, but with our hearts? To become engaged in a life which allows us to see things not just as they are, but also as they might be in the Kingdom that is advancing? Scripture is full of such invitations to reflect and become involved in the story.

See the support

The story found in 2 Kings 6 is a good example of reflecting about things that are beyond our normal senses. The servant of the prophet Elisha gets up early in the morning. He is expecting just another day. Perhaps he is yawning and rubbing the sleep from his eyes. He looks around and then rubs his eyes again. As he scans the horizon he is confronted by an awful truth. They are completely surrounded by the Syrian army. Soldiers ready for battle, chariots and horses. This is big trouble. The servant goes to Elisha to ask what they are going to do. They had been in scrapes before, but this was a tight spot.

Elisha turns to the servant and says, 'Don't be afraid, those who are with us are more than those who are with them.'

The servant must think that the prophet has finally lost it. As far as he can see this is obviously not true. The servant can see how many people are with Elisha and it is definitely not an army. He can see and hear their own fear. If he wanted, he could check whether they were shaking in their boots. With all this information he knew that there was more on the side of the Syrian army than on the side of the prophet. His disbelief was obviously evident to Elisha, who then prays for the servant.

'O Lord, open his eyes that he may see.' (verse 17)

Directly following the prayer the servant is able to see another army. This army is also full of horses and chariots but they are of fire. It is clearly an army of the Lord, sent to protect Elisha.

The servant has been enabled to glimpse a world beyond that which he could detect normally with his senses. He is given a fuller picture of what was taking place. Through the prayer of Elisha and God's answer to it, the servant is taken beyond his own narrow confines of reality and understanding, and enters the real world. He is being called to see the world differently, and to live in that difference. It would have been easy to rush around trying to search for an escape route, never seeing past the Syrian army and the huge fear that they must have caused. However, the prophet enabled the servant to stop, ponder and see what God was doing, opening up to him new possibilities for living.

Powerpoint – We are called to see the world differently and live in the difference.

Enter the world of faith

A favourite teaching method of Jesus was to tell stories that drew people into new worlds. As the master-teacher Jesus was able to give familiar settings, and yet as people were engaged in the stories they found themselves challenged to think or live in a new way.

Jesus invited people to picture scenes and circumstances and to use their imaginations to discover exciting and challenging possibilities. Let's look at a couple of examples.

We had just finished our evening meal. It had been a long hot day, and I was glad to sit and get my breath. I talked to the children for a while before they went to bed. I looked forward to spending time with my wife as she mended the children's clothes. All of a sudden there was a commotion outside.

'Daniel, Esther, are you there?'

It was our neighbour, Rhoda. I leapt up from my chair and rushed to the door.

Rhoda was a quiet widow woman and I knew that something must be wrong. I opened the door. She stood there, out of breath with a strange look on her face. She didn't look frightened; in fact I would say she appeared to be elated.

'What's the matter Rhoda? Are you all right? What has happened?' As I asked the question I ushered her into the house.

'Daniel, Esther, my friends,' she said, 'you must come to my home and celebrate with me.'

'Celebrate? What are you talking about? Do you feel all right, what has happened Rhoda?'

'Come.' She took our hands, and as I stared at her I saw that her eyes were glistening as a small tear made its way lazily down her face.

We were now captivated and wanted to know what had happened. What had caused this state in our neighbour? When we went next door there were a few other friends sitting all looking confused and desperate to hear Rhoda's tale.

Rhoda sat in the centre of the room and began to tell her story.

'Just before I got married, my father took me into a room so that he could talk to me. I was very nervous.' Rhoda looked at us and smiled, 'Just as I am now.'

She gave a little cough and continued with her story: 'My father took my hands in his and told me that he loved me and that he was grateful to God for me. I was stunned. I always felt that my father had wanted a son, and that I was a huge disappointment to him. He then let my hands fall as he turned towards his wooden chest. He bent down and lifted the heavy wooden lid up and reached inside. He took out a small silk bag. Then he turned back to me and opened the back.

'This was your mother's,' he said softly. 'She was beautiful, just like you.'

He opened out my hands and tipped out the contents of the back into them. I was stunned as it was the most beautiful thing that I had ever seen. I couldn't believe my eyes. It was a headband made of ten silver coins.

'This is my gift to you. When you look at it always remember where you came from.'

'I now store the headband in my own wooden chest, in a corner underneath some of my favourite clothes. When I feel down or frightened I go the chest and take out the silver jewellery and remember the love that was given to me in this gift.

'But last night I felt very sad. It is difficult to be alone. I did not sleep well and decided to take out the coins that remind me of who I really am. It was early and I took out the bag from the corner of the chest. I went to the corner of the room and sat, ready to remember. I put out my hand, just as my father had done all those years ago. The headband slivered out of the bag and right away I knew something was wrong.'

Rhoda stopped for breath and to regain her composure. We were all captivated, and everyone was still. We could not imagine what had happened, and we waited eagerly to hear the conclusion of the story.

'It took me a few moments to realize that one of the coins was missing. At first I thought that I must have made a mistake. Surely I must have miscounted. I started to panic. Surely I couldn't have lost it. What a failure I was. Stupid old woman that I am, I sat and cried.'

As we looked on she began to cry again. Tears raced one another down her face as she sobbed, remembering how badly she felt. So much of her life was encapsulated within that one piece of beautiful craftsmanship. Rhoda regained control and carried on.

'I knew at once that I must have dropped one of the coins the last time that I had taken the headband out, and had not noticed when I put it away. That was about a week ago, and I feared that it was lost forever. Then I thought that it must still be in the house. I searched, as I never had before.

'I looked in all the obvious places, but with no joy. Then I wondered if it had rolled into a crevice in the floor or into the wall. We all know how hard it is to see things in these houses so I got a lamp and looked in every corner. As I did I said a silent prayer that God might be merciful to me. Just when I had given up I thought that I saw a reflection, or a glimmer of something unusual. I was on my knees and I crawled over. There, in a small gap near the door, I saw the coin. I just sat there thanking God. I could hardly move. Somehow it felt as if I had my life back. I gently moved my hand down and picked it up. My heart leapt and I wanted to dance.'

Rhoda was in tears again but this time the tears were accompanied with laughter. We all started to laugh with her. We all rejoiced with her. She had lost something precious to her and now it was found.

'Now I have all my special coins again, at last I can rejoice.'

The parable of the 'Lost Coin' is found in Luke 15. Jesus concludes the story by saying that, 'There is rejoicing in the presence of the angels of God over one sinner who repents' (verse 10). Jesus only takes a few minutes to give a brief outline of a story full of emotion and poignancy. He does so to allow his hearers to glimpse another reality, the reality that is the joy in heaven among angels at the repentance of a sinner. This highlights the reality of the value that God places on the lost. The truth is that God has a missionary heart. It is the invitation from Jesus to glimpse at how God views things. Jesus has enabled people to use their imagination to discover spiritual truth. He is the master communicator and the greatest storyteller of all time. I wonder if Jesus were telling parables in our area tomorrow, would we make the time to listen?

Just keep the plates spinning

For many of us the pace of life just gets faster and faster. No matter how much we get done there always seems to be more to do. The list of 'to do's' never seems to get any smaller. This constant rush leads to key characteristics in our lives. One is that everything has to happen now. We don't have time to wait on anything. We have to live for the moment. We use the microwave to heat up our coffee because we have no time to wait, or we drop by the local coffee house for our early wake up cappuccino. We run back to the car and then head to the first meeting.

If we've got children we drop them at nursery complete with pack lunch crammed into the box at the last minute. We are asked to do more at work than we used

to, and just when we work out the new computer programme someone else loads a new one. Then we rush
back to pick up the kids. Rush home and open the
freezer and scan the instant foods. We stick it in the
microwave and watch the food going round and
round, willing it to move faster. After all that has been
completed we crash out on the couch, glass in hand,
drifting off to sleep to the background mantra of some
talk show.

We also spend a lot less time with other people than
we used to. Many of us can go the whole day without
having a meaningful conversation with another human
being. Imagine a life with no listening or laughing, no
shared experiences. Now we can order our groceries
over the net and have them delivered. We can book holidays, review books and download music. In fact we can
do just about everything without leaving the house. Yet
is that really living? The community structures of a
bygone day have almost completely broken down. Some
of us can't even name our neighbours. It is always sad
when there is a newspaper report highlighting the death
of someone who has been lying on the floor for weeks,
and nobody has even noticed that they are missing.
Nobody has missed them, they haven't left an impres-
sion on anybody, and it appears that nobody cared. The
pace of life has robbed us of something precious: our
interdependence.

> **Powerpoint** – The pace of life has robbed us of some-
> thing precious, our need of one another.

Another problem with the rush of life is that our value
is based on what we produce. Worth is dependent on
what we do or what we earn, not what we are. We

must continue to do things in order to prove that we have any significance. Success is based on what we achieve, therefore we try to achieve more and more so that we feel as though we are worth more as people. No time to stop, no time to reflect, we have got to keep on keeping on. If Jesus were here to share a parable we would want him to cut to the chase. Get to the point. To stop and reflect and have our imaginations stretched would be too much of a nuisance to us. If Jesus could simply e-mail us with some bullet points that would be a great help. Then we could scan them if we got a minute and e-mail back if we had any questions.

Powerpoint – If Jesus could just e-mail us with bullet points that would be a great help.

This constant rush dictates our whole life. Like a circus entertainer we rush around trying to keep all the plates spinning. All our energy is spent preventing our lives from crashing around us, and being shattered into tiny pieces. This attitude crosses over into our spiritual lives. Often our spiritual lives are characterized by rush. Somewhere, in the tornado that is our early morning we try to fit in some reading, prayer and reflection. This 'quiet time' is taken somewhere between putting on your shoes and finding the car keys. We get the few verses read, tell God the things that we need and rush out of the door. In our minds we tick off the spiritual bit and get on with the real world.

Powerpoint – Have we rushed right by Jesus as we run out the door?

Some days we are so rushed that we never get round to praying at all. We have a great deal in common with Martha in the incident that is told in Luke 10. Jesus visits two sisters, Martha and Mary. They are friends of Jesus. He comes to them and provokes two responses. Martha ran around, wanting to get things right. She just worked herself into the ground. As she worked she got more and more annoyed with her sister who just sat at Jesus' feet and listened to him. Martha complained to Jesus and caught the response.

'You are worried and upset about many things, but only one thing is needed. Mary has chosen what is better, and it will not be taken away from her' (verse 42).

Sometimes rushing around getting things done is not appropriate. Yet it seems to be a mark of the way we live our lives. Is it any wonder that many of us feel that we are missing out on something in life? Is it that we have no peace and no sense of the presence of God?

We all know what it's like on a Sunday morning. We dive into the car ten minutes before the service begins to start the fifteen-minute drive. We snap at the kids. Why is it that children are always at their worst on Sunday mornings? We warn them in the church car park about their behaviour. Then we put on our Christian smile and jog into the building. Even as we enter we have in mind all the people that we have to connect with. That mental list of 'to do's' comes out again. New initiatives to hear about, notes to pick up. A couple of hours later we are back in the car and heading for lunch. We have heard a lot of voices, but not God's. The idea of entering into another world is beyond our experience. Perhaps on a good day we stop and think but we never imagine.

Powerpoint – In our minds we tick off the spiritual part and then get on with the rest of our real lives.

Explore new worlds, it's worship time

As a body the church has often not helped its various parts reflect and imagine. Order and control have been our primary interests. In order to keep control the leadership has stifled reflection. Teaching and understanding have attention over everything else. We tend to cram services with words. Perhaps we are scared of the unknown and wary of silence.

For me the Lord's Supper service is a great example of this. We come to a table that points us to the past, present and future – to what Jesus has done, what he is doing and what he will do. It takes us afresh to the suffering love of Jesus and the amazing sacrifice for us. It calls us to spiritually gaze upon the horror and wonder of the finished work of Jesus on the cross. It also makes us reflect on the present. How do we respond as individuals and as a community of believers to such wonderful love? It is the challenge and the encouragement of God's salvation outworking in us. It touches our hearts, and should affect our lives as we come afresh to God. It also gives a glimpse of that final consummation of the Lord and his church. That time when people of every tribe, tongue and nation will be with him forever, lost in wonder and adoration. If ever there is a time to reflect and imagine then this is it. This is the moment to see the way in which God's Kingdom has broken through, showing us that life need never be the same again. Yet, in my experience these services are often the ones that are most tightly organized and controlled. We must know who will serve who, which rows will be called to the front first, and what type of bread and wine we should be using.

> **Powerpoint** – Sometimes we have to let go and allow God to do surprising things.

If we have a clear order then we can keep control and nothing unexpected can really happen. Surely we need to make space and allow people the time to reflect upon the glory of God. As we come to God, we should expect the unexpected to happen. Our worship should allow us to glimpse the world as it is in God, to re-imagine the difference that God has made in Jesus Christ. To provide for the whole community the alternative to the world in which we are living. Often we are content in making our services go well rather than go dangerously. We minister the mundane and add a Christian gloss to a non-Christian lifestyle, rather than opening up the imagination of the community to see a kingdom world which is radically different to the one that we often feel chained to.

One last thought on all our rushing around. It is so easy to miss what God has placed right in front of us. In Luke 12 we have Jesus teaching his disciples and he highlights the need to slow down and reflect. In the King James version the word used is 'consider'. I like it because it makes me want to stop and take time out to think. Think about these two verses:

'Consider the ravens; for they neither sow nor reap; which neither have storehouse nor barn; and God feedeth them: how much more are ye better than the fowls.' (verse 24)
'Consider the lilies how they grow' (verse 27)

There is so much spiritual truth around us, but we never stop long enough to see it. When was the last time you stopped to consider the flowers and wondered at the goodness of God? I love the way *The Message* paraphrases these verses: 'Look at the ravens, free and unfettered, not tied down to a job description carefree in the care of God...Walk into the fields and look at the wildflowers. They don't fuss with their appearance – but have you ever seen colour and design like it?'[1]

Like children we have the opportunity to enter into this world beyond our senses, to take the hand of God and step out into the unknown. We can reflect and think upon what that kingdom means to our lives and the lives of others. The possibility is for leaders to become artists and poets instead of managers. For us there is the possibility to glimpse the limitless possibilities that are ours in Christ.

Reflection

What will it be like?

The spotlight hits you. You are at the centre and every eye is drawn to you. I know that I am part of a huge crowd but it feels to me as if we are alone. Only you and I. Standing before you everything makes sense. Finally, I am free. Free from pain, sorrow, tears and death. Now I can worship you with untainted love.

How can I find appropriate praise to give you Lord?

Rosebuds; pink gentle petals at your feet, your blood-stained feet.

Oil, warm and sweat to anoint your brow, your thorn-gashed brow.

Gold, silver rings to adorn your pierced hands.

There is nothing that is appropriate. All I can offer is who I am and what I have become in your grace.

Action

Take thirty minutes in a park or garden. Look around and reflect. What does the beauty of nature tell you about the care of God?

Read a story that Jesus told. Reflect upon it. Dwell on the way in which Jesus draws hearers into stories to teach spiritual truth. Try and get a glimpse of the alternative life that Jesus has called you into. What would it take in your life to make time to go with God into new possibilities?

Pause for a short time of silence.

Dear God, you are the great artist.
You speak and create; you move and open up new horizons.
Help me to go with you into uncharted new lands.
Help me to be less busy and more open to you.
In the lovely name of Jesus I pray,
Amen.

---

[1] Eugene Peterson, *The Message*, p. 180

5

Becoming a risky person to know

The risk taker

I am so timid. The idea of stepping out is one that fills me with dread. Especially in my spiritual and church life. I like to be comfortable and contented. However, I have a feeling that this desire for always being secure and safe has meant that I have missed out on a lot in my relationship with Jesus. In hindsight I have recognized that God has opened many doors for me that I have refused to go through. There have been opportunities to grow and develop that my timidity has hindered. I wonder how many relationships of blessing have passed me by because I have not had the confidence to reach out and move towards others. Often, I have felt more like a spectator than a participant, a supporter instead of a player.

In church, there are lots of people like me, preferring safety to risk. But is that the life we have been called to in God? I believe that we are called by a risk-taking God to join the band of risk takers that he leads. Sometimes God leads us into the unknown but he never leaves us alone. In this chapter we will explore the place of risk-taking in our spiritual lives, to try and determine just what it would take for us to move out of the comfort zone and on in the journey of adventure with God.

> **Powerpoint** – How many opportunities for blessing have we missed because we have been too timid?

The supermarket sweep

It was a cloudy cold morning. I had a feeling that doing grocery shopping on a Saturday was not going to be a good idea. Normally we go to our local supermarket on a Monday morning when it is quiet and relaxed. On a Monday shopping can be an almost stress-free environ- ment but I had a sneaky suspicion that Saturday would be totally different. As soon as we got to the car park I knew that I had been correct. It was packed with cars being driven around by manic men or grumpy grans desperately trying to find a space as close to the store as possible. My older son Jonathan had decided not to come with us, a decision of wisdom beyond his years.

Eventually, we found a space for the car and headed towards the supermarket. It is hard to decide what I like least about the shop. Is it the artificial lighting, the music or just the crowds? We went through the automatic doors and wandered into the 'fruit and veg' section.

'What difference does it make what type of mush- rooms we buy?' I moaned to my wife.

'I guess you're just not a fungi,' she said.

It was then that I noticed the toddler. He had a mop of blond curly hair. He had a little white cardigan on and green cord trousers. He was going as fast as his lit- tle legs could carry him. His mum had made the fatal mistake of taking her eyes away from him and on to the apples. He saw his chance and made a break for it. A cute side step got him between an older couple and their trolley. However, just as he glimpsed freedom, a maternal hand was placed on his shoulder. He was then whisked up into the child seat in the trolley, and he let everybody in the aisle know what had happened.

It was an entertaining interruption to the tedium before we headed towards the 'soups and world rice' section. We weaved our way from aisle to aisle without any great mishaps and no permanent damage to feet or ankles. As we waited in the queue at the checkout a message came over the tannoy.

'Could the parents of Jamie please come to the information desk to collect your child.'

I looked along to the desk and there they were – the same mum and little boy with the mop of blond hair. It was clear that he had tried again. With the spirit of a prisoner of war tunnelling towards freedom he had seen the chance and taken the risk. Weighing up the pros and cons was not for him; rather he saw the chance and went for it. I wondered how many children a day ended up at the information desk. Each having been driven by a determination to see beyond where they were and leaving everything behind in the charge for what was around the next corner.

On the way back to the car I pondered the joy on the small boy's face as he ran down the aisle. That mixture of freedom, fun and risk. Is it any wonder that God loves children?

Little guy with a big problem

'David, David hurry I have an important job for you to do.'

I ran straight away, immediately recognizing my father's voice. Things had been really busy here. There was always a lot of work to do and three of my brothers were away with the army. Mostly, my job was to care for the sheep. Shepherd David, they called me, but I didn't mind. Sometimes it could get quite exciting up there in the mountains. Sometimes there would be a bear or a lion on the prowl, and I would have to protect any strays. Keeping the sheep from harm, that was my job.

I wondered what my dad wanted me to do. I stood quietly before him awaiting instructions. He looked up at me with tired eyes and a weary expression.

'I am worried about your brothers,' he said, 'we haven't heard anything from the front for so long. These boys get caught up in the adventure and forget those of us left at home. I want you to go to the front. You are to take roasted grain and bread for the boys. We all know what army food is like, and they must keep up their strength for the battle. I have also packed up some cheeses for the commander. See that he gets them. Go directly to the camp, give them the food and find out what you can. I am anxious for news.'

'And David,' I looked up, 'make sure you come right back. No daydreaming and no carry on, do you understand?'[1]

I got my gear together and headed for the camp. I wondered what it would be like. Some of the other boys had been talking, and had said that the Philistines had a great army. They were camped on a hillside at the Valley of Elah. Our troops were on the other side of the canyon. Some said that our army might be in trouble. But I knew that we would win against any enemy because God was on our side. If God was for us then nobody could defeat us. The Philistines didn't scare me. We were the people of God, and we could face any enemy in his name.

So I travelled to the camp without any mishaps. It was bigger than I imagined. It was dusty and noisy, and, I must admit, a little frightening. There was a loud war cry and most of the army were getting ready to go out and take up their positions. I spoke to a soldier who was running past me.

'Do you know where the tents of Eliab, Abinadab and Shammah are?'

He stopped and scowled at me. 'Who are you? And why do you want to know? An army camp is no place for a boy like you. Go home to your mother.'

With that he moved on. What a cheek! I knew that I could do as much as he was doing. I nearly shouted after him but thought better of it.

Eventually I found the supply tent and left the food supplies there. Then I went looking for my brothers. I ran along the battle-lines until I got a glimpse of them. I shouted and waved.

'Eliab, Abinadab, Shammah, it's me, David.'

They looked up with a mixture of surprise and embarrassment. We hugged one another. Then Eliab spoke up. 'What are you doing here? You should be at home watching the sheep.'

I was really annoyed at him. He always thinks he knows best just because he is the oldest.

'Instead of going on at me I thought you would have wanted to know how dad was. He sent some extra food for you. I travelled all this way with it. Not that I'm likely to get any thanks from you.'

Just then there was a stirring in our ranks. I looked up to see what was going on. All eyes were focused upon the Philistine camp. There walking towards us was a huge soldier. When I say huge I mean *enormous*. He was getting closer and started shouting at our troops. It was hard to make out what he was saying but whatever it was, it had an effect on our army. You could almost hear them shaking. This giant was covered from head to toe in armour, and he had another soldier running in front of him carrying a shield. He was a pretty awesome sight and it was enough for our soldiers as they turned and ran back to camp.

I was embarrassed and annoyed. Imagine the army of the people of God running. O I know that he was big but what was that to us? Is anyone more powerful than our God? As I talked to my brothers I found that this giant from Gath had offered a challenge everyday for forty days but nobody was willing to fight him.

I couldn't believe that we were cowering away like frightened rabbits as God's name was being mocked. Then I heard that the king had offered a reward package to anyone who fought and defeated the giant, who I was told was called Goliath. I asked some of the soldiers around what this package was. It was while I was discussing these things that the argument happened. Eliab became really nasty. Ever since the prophet Samuel came to our house, Eliab has had it in for me. Yet this time he was really nasty. He bombarded me with questions right in front of all the soldiers.

'Why did you really come here? Whom did you leave the sheep with? I know how wicked your heart is. You are conceited and just came to see the battle.'

I don't know why he said what he did. Maybe he was embarrassed by my questions. It was really hard to stand there and listen to him. I knew that everyone was looking at me. I was sweating and must have had a face like a beetroot. I felt like pushing him or shouting at him but just as I was about to do something, I realized that my energy was needed fighting Goliath, rather than my own brother. It was more important to me that God was being mocked. What does it matter what anyone else thought about me? It was as I considered these things that I got an unexpected call. The king wanted to see me. King Saul had a royal tent from where he governed the plans for the army, though there didn't really seem to be much of a plan at the moment. Maybe the plan was for the army to run away everyday. Perhaps it was to lull them into over self-confidence.

The king was obviously desperate for someone to go and fight. He had offered great wealth, a tax-free life and marriage into the royal family as rewards. Pretty good offers, but these did not motivate me. My main motivation was the glory of my God, and the honour of his name.

As soon as I saw the king, I told him not to despair. I would go out and fight the giant. At first I don't think that he believed me. I was only young, and not even a member of the army. If hardened soldiers were too frightened to do anything, what could a young shepherd boy do? Goliath was a professional killer, a tough soldier used to bloodshed and violence. I tried to reassure the king that I was not afraid. I had overcome the odds before. On various occasions I had encountered frightening things while tending the sheep. I had faced a roaring lion that was ready to have me for lunch, and I had encountered a hungry and angry bear keen to devour my sheep. Each time I could have been killed, but I knew that the Lord had been with me, and that his power would always sustain and protect me.

I am not sure why he agreed. I think it was because he was so desperate. Whatever the reason, the king agreed. Perhaps it was only when he said OK that I began to realize just what I had let myself into. It was a big risk, and making a laughing stock of myself might be the least of my problems. There I was, a young boy, not trained to fight, never been to war against a trained killer. On the other hand Goliath's very name was a byword for ruthlessness. Even the toughest of our soldiers were scared to face him. Yet I knew that my God was able to protect me. His honour was all that was important.

I told the king, 'The Lord who delivered me from the paw of a lion and the paw of the bear will deliver me from the hand of this Philistine.'

The next thing that I knew the king ordered some of his men to dress me. They put a tunic on me, and then this huge coat of armour and a big bronze helmet on my head. I felt absolutely ridiculous. Everything was so big, and as I tried to walk, I staggered about as if I was drunk. They gave me a sword to fasten around my waist. Well that was the final straw. As I moved around, I could tell that the soldiers had to work really hard not to burst out laughing. It was clear to everybody that I had never worn anything like this before. It was all so awkward and slow. Rather than protect me, I would be a sitting duck. The only chance that I might have would be if Goliath came out, marched to the front, saw me standing and laughed himself to death.

'This is just stupid,' I said, 'I can't wear this. I know that you are just trying to help but I will have to do it my way and trust in the Lord for protection.'

I could see the soldiers looking at one another as if to say that I had gone completely mad. Saul just shrugged his shoulders and ordered the men to help me back out of all the gear. It was clear to me that some of them didn't think I was taking a risk. They thought I was heading into some hopeless venture that was going to end in my death.

The king hugged me as I left his tent. As I walked passed my brothers, I think I detected a tear in the eye of Abinadab. I wanted to stop and talk, and tell them how I felt, but I knew that if I stopped now I might never be able to start again. I smiled at them and just kept walking. I left the camp and headed down to the stream. I felt very warm, and the sweat trickled down into my eyes making them sting. Around the edge of the water I started to search. I knew exactly what I was looking for. Smooth stones. They had to be the right size for my sling, and they had to be hard. It was as if someone had placed exactly the right stones all along the stream's edge. I picked up about a dozen and then inspected them. I threw some away and was left with the best five. The water looked so cool and inviting.

I sat for a few seconds, thinking of my father and my family, and as I looked out on the water I remembered that my God was able to part the seas. God had never failed us before. Surely he would not fail us now. It is difficult, even now, to explain how I felt at that moment. Suddenly I had a sense that God was with me. I was still scared but had a peace in my heart. There was no more time to waste; I got up, put the stones in my pouch and went to face the giant.

It seemed to be very still, as if the whole world held its breath. I looked up to see them approaching. The closer the giant got the more frightening he became. He was so tall that I thought the sun would be blocked out behind him. When he saw me he started to laugh. Then he mocked me.

'Is this the best that the Israelites can do, a stupid little boy? Have you all got so scared that you hide behind a baby?' As he spoke he looked with a real hatred in his eyes. 'Well, if this is all you have I will just have to take it. You will hear his screams right across the valley. Is this the best your God can do? A God who relies upon children? He's not worth worshipping.'

Then looking down towards me he spat and then said in a low voice, 'You're going to die little boy.'

My throat was very dry. I could taste the sweat as it cascaded down my face and hung on my lips. I knew I had to say something. I could not let this Philistine mock my God,

'You come against me with sword and a spear and a javelin, but I come against you in the name of the Lord Almighty the God of the Armies of Israel whom you have defiled. He will hand you over to me.'

My legs felt really heavy and my heart was beating so loud that I could hear it, but I knew that it was now or never. I ran towards him. I think that shocked him. He was in for a bigger shock. I reached in to my little pack, pulled out a stone and slung it as hard as I could. I don't know where the strength came from, but that stone really shifted. As it left the sling I said a silent prayer for the Lord to save his people and reveal the power of God. The stone hit him right in the middle of the head. He staggered. I think he was as much shocked as hurt, but then he floundered and crashed to the ground. I stood for a few seconds. All my energy seemed to leave me. I remember faintly hearing cheers from the army behind me. The giant that had brought fear and dread into all these hearts had been defeated by a small boy who trusted in a great big God and took a risk in him.

Powerpoint – God is able to defeat our giants of fear.

A wider picture

Wherever you look in the Bible you are faced with risk takers. Humanly speaking Jesus was the great risk taker. If you were calling people to follow you would you have picked the disciples? Tax collectors, fishermen, radicals and the traditional all made up Jesus' inner circle. There were people who were ambitious, longing to see a new order come. Others just seem to have been plain confused. Some spoke up and others talked among themselves.

Imagine leaving that group to develop the Church and take the gospel into the world. If you or I were planning a world-wide strategy to share the most important message in the history of language, I think we would have been a bit more choosy. The charismatic personality, or the leading academic would have swayed us. Experience would be vital, and we would have wanted three references. Applicants would have needed to take a personality test to check their mental stability.

For us style and substance would have to knit together in the proposed candidate. If the person we wanted was of influence, so much the better. I don't think that any of the people that Jesus called would have made our short list. What a great comfort that is. God did not call just the perfect, the beautiful or the obviously gifted. God continues to delight in taking risks with people. God calls and encourages the weak, ordinary and, in the world's eyes, the totally unremarkable. God takes risks on people like you and I. However, are we willing to take risks in our walk with God?

Powerpoint – God delights in taking the shabby and vulnerable and turning them into the beautiful.

It was not just with the calling of the disciples that Jesus took risks. Chatting to the Samaritan woman broke down generations of suspicion and prejudice. Even the disciples were shocked to find Jesus talking to this woman. Yet after the woman had her life-changing encounter with Jesus, she then went back into her village to tell others about him. With her reputation it must have taken some courage from her to share with those who were her neighbours. Whatever she said it must have been powerful because a lot of people came to the well in the middle of the day to see Jesus for themselves. They were so keen to hear the message that Jesus was sharing that they convinced him to stay for another two days.

As they listened to him they realized for themselves that Jesus was the Saviour of the world. John's account of the story goes on to tell us that, 'Because of his words many more became believers. They said to the woman, 'We no longer believe just because of what you said; now we have heard for ourselves, and we know that this man really is the Saviour of the world.' (Jn. 4: 42)

Jesus took a risk by sharing God's love with this outsider. She then took a risk by going back to the village and sharing her testimony with people who knew all about her past failures. Through that stepping out by the woman, many folk from the village believed for themselves.

Jesus continually took risks with men and women. Touching those that others would never go near. Challenging others who felt morally superior.[2] Driven by the higher calling of the love of God, Jesus refused to be confined by the rules and regulations of his culture. Love was always the momentum behind Jesus' actions, and love propelled him into the unknown and difficult areas of life.

Powerpoint – Love propels us into the business of taking risks.

When people that God takes risks on start to trust him
then amazing things can happen. Think about some of
the people in the New Testament and in the history of
the church. People that the world would never look
twice at were able to do amazing feats of goodness and
courage because of their ability to step out and trust in
the power and greatness of God. Let's think of some of
them and take time to be encouraged by ordinary people who trusted in an extraordinary God.

> **Powerpoint** – Amazing things happen when people
> become risk takers.

A bad reputation

It must have been an amazing experience to be involved
in leadership in the early church. Sitting in Jerusalem
hearing what the Holy Spirit had been doing must have
been so exciting. The church at Antioch was really
buzzing, things were happening in amazing ways. In
Acts 11 Luke tells us 'a great number of people believed
and were turning to the Lord' (verse 21). It was clear that
the presence of the Lord was with them. God's grace
was changing things in such a powerful way that news
got back to the leaders of the church who were based at
Jerusalem. They were hearing bits and pieces, but didn't
seem to have a real picture of what God was doing. They
decided that things would need to be checked out and
authenticated.

In order to do this they would have to send someone
down to check it out and report back. They choose
Barnabas, a man who was trusted and respected by the
leadership. He was a man who was full of the Holy
Spirit. He was also a great encourager of others. What a

person to send to a young church where people were coming to faith and needed help to develop and strength their faith.

Barnabas headed for Antioch in Syria. It must have been a thought-provoking trip. It was three hundred miles from Jerusalem to Antioch. We don't know whether Barnabas had been to Antioch before, but he would have known all about it. Antioch was the third biggest city in the Roman Empire. It was a place with a large Jewish community, and at the time of the death of Stephen, many Christians fled to Antioch3. What would await this servant of Christ when he got to Antioch?

When he arrived he was thrilled by all that God was doing. Many people were finding faith; others were growing in understanding. Barnabas also knew that with the growth would come many problems. Some would drift away due to the pressure of others. Some would find it hard to change their lifestyles. Still others would become discouraged. Barnabas spent a lot of time sharing the gospel and encouraging new disciples to keep walking with the Lord. However, he knew that if the church was going to grow, it would be built upon teaching and leadership. People needed to be grounded in the basics of the faith. It was at that point that Barnabas showed himself to be a real risk taker. He decided that what the church required at this vital stage in its life was Paul. Paul, that man who had helped persecute the early church. The same Paul, who had been blinded by the risen Lord on the road to Damascus.[4] It was rumoured that he had been miraculously converted and was now a believer, but nothing much had been heard of him since.

Can you imagine the look on the faces of those in the church when Barnabas told then that he was going to find and bring back Paul? What a shock it must have been. Had Barnabas gone mad? Maybe he had been out in the sun for too long. Imagine those who had fled Jerusalem because of the persecution, now hearing that one of the chief persecutors was going to be invited to teach in the church. That must have been a sticky time for Barnabas, but he knew what the church needed and so he went for it. There would have been a million reasons for not asking Paul. A number of huge reservations would have been voiced, but Barnabas was able to see beyond all of these to envisage the right thing that was to be done.

> **Powerpoint** – There is always a million reasons for not stepping out but sometimes we have to go with what we know is right.

Barnabas headed for Tarsus to seek out Paul, giving him the opportunity to use and develop his gifts. Not only did Barnabas take a risk in his own leadership, he also took a chance on someone else. He was not disappointed; God was to use Paul mightily in the growth of the church at Antioch and far beyond. There must have been huge suspicion of Paul when he arrived in Antioch. People's reputations always go before them. However, for the next year both Barnabas and Paul worked tirelessly with the church teaching new converts and building a foundation for the church to grow and develop[5]. After that year there was a team of prophets and leaders, and God called Paul and Barnabas to leave the church and take the gospel into other areas. Following the call of the Holy Spirit the church blessed them and sent them out as missionaries into the world.[6] The church had been richly blessed because Barnabas was willing to take a risk by bringing a man with the bad reputation to the church.

A second chance

I have often wondered if Paul remembered the risk that Barnabas had taken in bringing him into the life of the congregation at Antioch. Paul was certainly willing to take a risk with others.

Paul was in prison going through a difficult time when he decided to write to Philemon. It was a personal letter of grace and care. Philemon was a wealthy member of the church, probably at Colosse. He had a slave called Onesimus who had run away from the house of Philemon, taking some things with him that did not belong to him. At some point he had come into contact with Paul while he was in prison. Onesimus had been converted and had become a great help to Paul. Indeed Paul clearly cares for Onesimus who he calls 'my very heart.'

Paul then takes a huge decision and a big risk. He could easily have just kept the slave with him. After all, he had been converted by Paul and was really useful to him. Surely, knowing the slave's reputation it would have been easier to keep an eye on him, checking that he was not tempted to stray from the faith and fall back into temptation. The hardest thing to do would be to send him back to the very place he ran from.

Of course there was an even bigger risk that Paul could take. He could write a letter asking Philemon to take the slave back. He could base it all on his own reputation and ministry. He could urge the church to regard Onesimus as a brother who would be a real blessing to the church. What a risk to take. If anything went wrong not only would Onesimus be blamed, but Paul too for urging the church to take him back. Paul was staking something of himself on this converted runaway.

Paul was putting his theology into practice. It was enough for him simply to write:

> 'He came and preached peace to you who were far away and peace to those who were near. For through him we both have access to the father by one Spirit. Consequently, you are no longer foreigners and aliens but fellow-citizens with God's people and members of God's household, built on the foundation of the apostles and prophets, with Christ Jesus as the chief cornerstone. In him the whole building is joined together and rises to become a holy temple in the Lord. And in Him you too are being built together to become a dwelling in which God lives by his Spirit.' (Eph. 2:17-22)

Paul also wrote in his letter to the Galatians that the Christian family is a new society, one that is miraculous and marvellous (Gal. 3: 26). The Message paraphrases Paul's words into 'In Christ's family there can be no division into Jew and non-Jew, slave and free, male and female. Among us you are all equal. That is, we are in a common relationship with Jesus Christ.'[7] To believe these things was wonderful but to act upon them was brave. That is what risk-taking is. To let our belief determine our actions, shaping who we are. Paul took the risk and believed that Onesimus had changed and would not fall back into his former mistakes. He also took the risk that the church was a loving growing new community who would welcome Onesimus as a brother. Paul took risks with himself, Onesimus, Philemon and the church. He did so because he believed in the greatness of God and the ability of God to change people and communities.

Powerpoint – Risk-taking is the practical application of our belief.

A tale of two cities

There are thousands of great examples of risk-taking in
the history of the church. This year two people particularly challenged me. They are separated by almost
everything – time, position, career – and yet they had
several things in common. They were people of courage,
and they stood up for what they knew to be right even
when they faced great opposition.

The weather was as unusual as a white tiger. It was so
warm I had to put on the air-conditioning on in the car.
The sky was cloudless, the clear blue of a gemstone. As
I drove along the country roads the trees on either side
stood tall. Silver birch, sycamore and oak remained
staunch but lifeless. The roads were almost free from
traffic as I past through the Yorkshire villages of Tunstal
and Roos. It seemed like a day from the past. I could
almost feel the tension slowly evaporate as the slow
pace of holiday time began to work its magic.

I drove to the outskirts of Hull and, after slowly
working my way through road works, I parked on the
edge of town. Leaving the car I started to walk to the
city centre. Traffic rushed by as I made my way across
the flyover. Stopping for a few seconds I gazed out to
see, and watched a large tanker make its way slowly
but definitely towards its unknown destination. The
day was getting warmer and I stopped to get a bottle of
water. As I took in the cool clear liquid I looked around
and saw a sign pointing towards the museum area of
the city. On entering the area a further sign pointed the
way to 'Wilberforce House'. William Wilberforce. In
the back of my mind a few ideas began to stir and
pushed themselves to the front. I knew that he had
been a politician who had fought for the abolition of
slavery. He had been a Christian who felt that his faith

had to be worked out through working for justice and compassion. Apart from these few sketchy ideas, very little else was clear to me. What a good chance to find out more. I turned right and headed for Wilberforce House.

The iron gates spoke of stability and history. A large old tree stood at the left of the front door adding to the sense of time and stability. Going through the front door I was met by a bright and helpful woman who pointed me to the rooms up the stairs that featured the life and work of Wilberforce. Climbing the wooden staircase, I stopped to gaze at large framed portraits of the great and the good. Entering into a large room filled with information and artefacts about his life, I began to picture the life of a great risk taker.

William Wilberforce was born in 1759. His family were wealthy and of good reputation and social standing. When he was only eight years old his father died and William faced various changes in his life. One of these was to be sent to live with his aunt. She was an influential and staunch Methodist and had several well-known friends. It was possible that as a boy William would have come into contact with George Whitefield, the famous evangelist, and the preacher and hymn-writer John Newton. It is hard to imagine the impact that his time with his aunt had upon him. Certainly, his mother was concerned about the impact that such spiritual fervour might have on him, and sent him to private school.

It was while he was at St John's College at Cambridge that William began a friendship with another William who was to become a famous politician. William Pitt the younger became Prime Minister, and it was his friendship and encouragement to Wilberforce that remained a constant strength.

The year 1784 was very significant for William Wilberforce. It was the year in which his life was changed forever. He had already been in Parliament as elected representative from Yorkshire for four years, but it was in 1784 that he became an evangelical Christian. This conversion changed his outlook on his life and role as a member of Parliament. He became interested in issues relating to poverty and justice. He became concerned with the reforming of the morals of society and he worked to put his faith into practice. He did not work alone but had fellowship and support from others.

Wilberforce and his friends became known as the Clapham Sect. They were named after a village south of London where a lot moved in evangelical Anglican circles. Most of them were busy professionals who gave both time and money working for social justice. They funded schools, worked for better working conditions in factories and fought to allow freedom to missionaries in India. It was their intention to live in ways that brought the love of God into the centre of their society. While they worked on all these issues together their greatest endeavour was to rid the nation of slavery.

Wilberforce was at the forefront of this campaign. He knew that it would not be easy. The campaign would encounter a lot of opposition from those in power. Indeed a lot of those associated with Wilberforce's own upbringing found his opinions to be quite shocking. Yet his heart was moved by the plight of those caught in the vice of slavery. British ships were carrying black slaves from Africa to the West Indies as goods to be bought and sold. Wilberforce was one of those who could not stand back and allow this to happen without saying or attempting to do something about it.

He was not the only one to think that way, but he was in a position to try and get the law changed. It was a big risk: he would be in direct conflict with many important and influential people. Much of the weight of the establishment would be focused upon him. His life would never be the same again, but he firmly believed that faith must be worked out in our actions.

In 1788 Wilberforce began his campaign in the House of Commons to have slavery abolished. There was great opposition, but Wilberforce would not be discouraged. Every year for the next eighteen years he would bring anti-slavery motions to Parliament, passionately campaigning for the end of slavery. Finally, in 1807 Wilberforce and many other Christians rejoiced as parliament voted to abolish the slave trade. However, Wilberforce recognized that there was still much more to do. He then pressed for the emancipation of all slaves held in the British colonies. He introduced a bill to Parliament. It was defeated. With typical enthusiasm he introduced it again and again, never giving up the fight for what he knew to be right. Years went by and the work continued. It was not until 1833, the year in which Wilberforce died that the Emancipation Bill finally became law.

For over forty years Wilberforce lived life as a risk taker. It cost him a great deal. He was threatened with death by opposition. He had a time of burnout and also witnessed the hounding and false accusations of his friends. However, he continued to the end, and God honoured that faithfulness.

I stood gazing out of a window in one of the rooms in the museum and considered the bravery that it took to stand up for what Wilberforce knew to be right. Even with support and encouragement it was a huge risk to become involved. He could have worked for a number of other good causes that would have never brought him into conflict nor cost him so much in terms of his privacy and social standing. However, for Wilberforce

to be a Christian was to serve God, embracing the cost
and making a difference. I felt greatly challenged as I
considered a comfortable life made uncomfortable for
the sake of the gospel. How many times had I turned
away from risk because I did not know where it would
lead? Perhaps it would have led to a deeper awareness
of the presence of God.

Powerpoint – Risk leads to greater fellowship with
Jesus, the great risk taker.

As I went back out into the bright sunshine two images
stayed with me. One was a copy of a political cartoon,
now held in the British Museum. It was an attempt to
undermine Wilberforce by claiming he was only interested in the issue of slavery because he kept African
mistresses. He was hounded and ridiculed but that was
part of the risk. Wilberforce knew that to follow Jesus
was not going to win him any popularity contests.
Being faithful always leads to being unpopular with
some people. What courage it must have taken to speak
up and keep speaking up for those who could not speak
up for themselves.

The other image was a model of a ship carrying
slaves. The museum had given us an insight into the
conditions below deck. It was a gruesome sight. People
were shoved together like matches in a box. Men,
women and children being used and abused like cheap
furniture. Pieces of cheap property with life cruelly
crushed from them.

Knowing the cost, he was willing to take the risk to
get the job done. It was through that risktaking that others gained courage and change slowly began to take
place.

Powerpoint – Our small risks may bring courage to others.

The idea of our risk taking being used by God to bring about change reminded me of a visit to another city and another museum.

Atlanta feels almost like a second home to me. I have travelled there often in the last three years as I studied for a Doctor of Ministry at Columbia Theological Seminary. Sitting on the 'Marta Train' I gazed at the map of the Marta routes posted upon the side of the train. Several people were sitting in their own worlds, lost in the sounds coming from their personal CD players. Each one seemed to be oblivious to all that was taking place around them. The train slowed down at the station. As we pulled into the station the voice came clearly through the carriages, 'King Memorial Station, depart from here for the King Centre.'

Coming out of the station the heat felt like a slap on the face and I grabbed my sunglasses as the brightness forced me to screw up my eyes. Following the directions I headed slowly through several streets until I turned the corner at Ebenezer Baptist Church. The church was built from 1914 to 1922. On 25 February 1948 Dr Martin Luther Junior was ordained and appointed as the associate pastor to work alongside his father, Rev Martin Luther King Senior. The church is important to the history of civil rights in America as many meetings were held to plan the strategy of non-violent direct action. There were many buses outside the church and I decided to move on to the King Centre.

There were several school parties. Under-pressure teachers were trying to make history live. It was a hard job. The children would much rather have been out in the sun than wander around a building, no matter how important the things in this building were.

It was great to glimpse both the naivety and enthusiasm of the children as they rushed from board to board and information card to information card like birds in a newly sown field. I stood and delighted in their joy of life. A young teacher looked and smiled as she tried to round up her charges.

As the children moved into another room I was able to slowly look around at glimpses of history. There were the robes and Bible of Martin Luther Junior, as well his aftershave and other personal items. Here also was the story of the life of a person and a movement. The life ended, but the example and the work carries on.

I left the room with a strange sense of sorrow and admiration. I ambled along the corridor and entered a smaller room. On the walls were various brightly coloured banners. They were rainbows of texture and colour. Made by local school and community groups, they were reflections on peace and freedom. I took my time to savour each one as if it they were part of a palatable special dinner. Each one was both appetising and fulfilling. Then my eyes were drawn to the picture of Rosa Parks. It is a picture that portrays a lady of courage and dignity.

It was the end of another busy day. The date was 1 December 1955. The small middle-aged seamstress slumped down into the seat on the bus. The bus was busy but Rosa got a seat in the section of the bus set apart for non-whites. She was tired and weary after a long day's work. Then, as the bus was about to get under way, a white man asked her to give up her seat. According to the law, this was his right. I am sure that this had happened to lots of people in the past. Many tired and weary people faced the indignity of having to give up their seat purely because of the colour of their skin.

On this day, this woman became a risk taker. Something in her said enough is enough, this far and no further. This day she was tired not just because of her long day of work; she was tired of the history of oppression.

There must have been a potent mixture of nervous energy and courage, faith and fear. In taking the risk of saying no, Rosa faced a great deal of opposition and stress, but God used her risk to the benefit of many others. When Rosa refused to give up her seat she was running through a God-given open door. The rest of the story is well-known; her arrest and trial, the role of Martin Luther King Junior and others, a bus boycott that lasted 381 days and finally the Supreme Court ruling that bus segregation was unconstitutional.

Her risk-taking was a catalyst for others to see the beginning of change. What many people don't know was the strong place that faith played in Rosa's life. She grew up in a home where the Bible and prayer were central to life. Everyday her grandmother would tell her Bible stories and her grandfather would pray. Rosa's belief in God and her convictions about the presence and help that God brings were central to all that she did.

Powerpoint – How important it is to be mentors of faith in our families.

I stood in the room oblivious to the enthusiasm of the children, lost in my own thoughts. It is amazing the ways in which God honours the courage of ordinary people. This woman of faith was used to alter the thinking of a nation. I turned and walked back down the stairs and decided not to go into the shop.

Stepping out of the building the heat of an Atlanta day hit me like a right hook from a heavyweight. More powerful than the sun was the image of a woman and her God standing against the forces of history and society. A woman who saw a risk and took it and in that stepping out, found a new strength and a belief that with God, we can all make a difference.

> **Powerpoint** – To risk with God is to go to the well of the waters of strength and renewal.

A risky community

It is far easier to talk about risk-taking than to do it. The society in which we live is becoming more secular by the second. The things of God are not high on anybody's agenda. To speak out is to stand out and risk both rejection and isolation. To face these things is a brave and difficult step. Yet it is the way of Jesus. To follow Jesus is to be willing to risk all for his sake.

In the church of our day, risk-taking is not one of the priorities for many congregations. Instead a great deal of our time is being spent on maintaining what we already have. Like the good-old-day entertainer we run from pole to pole spinning each plate trying to make sure that none of them crash to the ground. With fewer people to keep them spinning, we are hard pressed to think of anything else. It is so easy to dwell on the difficulties that we all endure. That is not to say that we should ignore or underestimate our difficulties. However, we must be careful that we do not neglect adventure, turning the Christian community into a frightened minority.

Powerpoint – We are a called community, not a frightened minority.

In such a climate preachers often urge church members on to greater effort, more faithfulness and determination. Like a first-class stamp, stickability becomes absolutely vital. There is nothing wrong with any of these things in themselves. However, as Christian communities we should be creating an atmosphere that encourages people to take risks. In our worship we must be enabling people to discern what the Spirit is doing and giving them the permission to step out.

This permission-giving is a vital part of the life of the community of faith. To send people out into the world to follow the call of God is part of our ministry. Each of us is called to be an encourager, giving people confidence to take risks because they know that we are alongside them. Whatever individuals face, they face it as part of the one body. Risk-taking should be prayed for and shared within the congregation's life. Do sharing and celebrating the opportunities that God is giving to us mark our community life?

Powerpoint – We need to give permission to our brothers and sisters to take risks.

At the heart of Christian community must be the taking of risks with one another. Becoming vulnerable and open with one another is a big step for many of us to take. Sometimes it can be a painful experience, yet it is part of the risk-taking of love that we are all called to become involved in.

> **Powerpoint** – Our faith stories could be a great bless-
> ing to others if we have the courage to share them.

Into the unknown

The church in which I minister is one born out of a risky
decision. I was minister of a church in the city centre of
Perth in Scotland. It was a church with a long history
and a proud tradition. However, the congregation was
growing old and tired. At the same time the area that the
church was called to minister to had changed fairly dra-
matically over the previous twenty years.

The church tried various ways to build bridges with
people in the wider community, but the gap was huge.
Many people in the church worked hard to get involved,
but the wider community was one of many needs and
the church had been marginalized in the thinking of
most. While the church was able to grow, those who
came did not live in the community. Mostly, they were
Christians moving into the area.

The church began to consider its future. Two things
struck most of the congregation: first they liked the
church as it was – it was safe and the order was one they
were comfortable with. Secondly they understood that
this model didn't work in reaching beyond ourselves.
What to do? We could either go on as we were for a
while or try to do something different.

The theme of the incarnation became central to much
of the conversation. Why are we trying to get people in
to a building, why don't we try to get out amongst people where they are? One possibility came to the fore. We
could close down and start again. We could allow people to find another traditional church that suited their
need and then start a new church in the heart of the

wider community. This would involve people taking a big risk. Members would have to vote the church out of existence. They would have to let go of many important things believing that God may do new things in the future. Even though they might not be part of this, they would still have to let go of the old.

After a lot of discussion, prayer and thought the congregation closed down and a new congregation, much smaller than the old began to meet in the local school. It meant thinking about church in new ways. It has been the start of a journey of discovery about God, ourselves and the world around us. It has challenged us to get alongside people who have never been part of any faith community. Church has become much more of a messy business, something between chaos and order, but in the midst of it all God has been at work. Lives are being transformed and a community is being built.

Many things have gone wrong. Sometimes we have been too quick; at other times we have been paralysed by fear and missed opportunities. Occasionally, we have bruised our spiritual shoulders, trying to push open closed doors. At other times we have failed to see that huge opportunities have been presented to us. Yet it has been in the stepping out that we have been challenged to trust God in the midst of the chaos. We are learning to delight in each step that we are helped to take by the great risk taker.

Powerpoint – There is a mix of fear, delight and growth as we step out in trust.

A day at the races

We all dived for the big bowl of popcorn that was sitting on the table. I lose out again and end up with a meagre handful. We sit back and watch one of the family's favourite films. The music starts, sounds of the jungle blast out, and the camera follows the group as they push their way through the trees. Suddenly as they trek onwards, one of the hired guides pulls a gun from his belt and is about to shoot the man at the front of the group. All of a sudden the leader turns and with a flick of the wrist a whip flashes, accurate and strong like a cobra striking at unsuspecting prey. The whip knocks the gun from the hand of the prospective killer, who flees as fast as he can, clutching to his chest his painful hand. The camera then focuses on the man with the whip. Unshaven and rough, and yet we all know that he is going to be the hero. In the next five minutes of the film he looks at a tattered map then heads forward with a confident stride; this is a man who knows what he wants.

Coming to an opening in the rocks he hardly takes a breath before plunging into the darkness. He encounters just about every scary thing imaginable: large spiders, poison darts, skeletons and concealed traps. Does he stop or think about turning back? Not at all. It seems that the harder things get, the better he likes it. There is no fear, no concern, no panic, just determination to get to the prize. Trouble doesn't hinder him rather it spurs him on to the prize. What a guy Indiana Jones is. What a risk taker.

The next day I visit a family who are part of our church. It takes a few minutes before the mum comes to the door.

'I'm really sorry,' she says, 'we were so engrossed in the film that we never noticed the bell. Come on through, I'll just go and put the kettle on. I don't know how people coped with wet summer days before the video was invented.'

I follow her into the sitting room where lying on the floor there are two young children. You could have heard a pin drop and my intrusion into the room didn't even provoke a twitch. I sat on the couch and tried to share in the joy that was obvious on the faces of the children who were so wrapped up in the film.

A young girl, a small dog and two fairly strange-looking characters are in conversation with a lion. The lion is wiping his eyes and explaining that he is a coward.

'I haven't any courage at all, in fact I even scare myself,' he tells the assembled crowd of apparent misfits. He then points out that he has tired eyes because he can't sleep. One of the other characters suggests that he count sheep. 'It doesn't work I get scared of them,' relates the cowardly lion. Then the lion bursts into song and has a couple of great lines. I can't help laughing as he sings, 'But I could show my prowess, be a lion not a mouse if I only had the nerve.' The lion then heads down the yellow brick road hoping to meet the Wizard of Oz who will make all things well.

A hero or a mouse

After finishing my visit I got into the car and headed for home. Driving along I began to reflect upon the films that I had seen a little bit of during the last two days. I don't think that I will ever be an Indiana Jones. There will always be a little bit of me that thinks 'what if?' I don't think that I will ever fully get to that place where I won't care about what the consequences might be. In any case I'm not tough and I don't suit designer stubble. There are times when fear almost capsizes my life. To be so single-minded and focused would never be easy. However, I felt a bit uncomfortable at the similarities between the lion and myself. Were there times in my spiritual life when I could really have shown my prowess if I had just kept my nerve? Had I missed huge opportunities to be a blessing and receive blessing because I failed to show sufficient courage?

Perhaps to become a risk taker is to ask for God to so work in my life that I have the courage I need to make the decisions that I should. Perhaps it will never make us heroes but it may change our lives and the lives of those that we know.

As that child runs down the aisle of the supermarket, they find that there is a sense of freedom and joy as well as risk as they rush on their unknown quest. The parent is just a few steps behind, ready to swoop them up in their arms. If the child had not taken the risk, they would not have known the joy of the parent's arms drawing them closer to their heart. Perhaps the blessing of stepping out in trust is to discover God wrapping us up in his warm embrace.

Powerpoint – To be a risk taker may lead us into a greater knowledge of the love of God.

Reflection

Be Bold.
I like mice Lord
But I don't want to be one.

I want to soar like an eagle or roar like a lion
Not cowering away in the corner, shaking with fear
Unnoticed by decision makers.

My voice should be clear,
A cymbal-calling people to decision
Not the slight squeak of anonymity.

Perhaps it will never be my role in life to be a lion.
Maybe I will never be a hero to others
But if I am to be a mouse,
Lord make me a bold one.

Question

Take time to think and pray these questions through.

1. In what areas of my life do I need to step out more with God?
2. Would I describe my spiritual life as one of timidity? If so why?

Prayer

Lord, in uncertainty and confusion make me trusting.
Give me the courage to reach out for your hand and step

boldly into the majestic sunlight of your presence.

Help me Jesus, to face new challenges, in life, love or service with confidence.

Help me to believe that around every new corner on the street of uncertainty the first person that I will meet is you.

Amen.

---

[1] See 1 Samuel 17
[2] See Luke 5: 12 and Matthew 19: 16
[3] See Acts 8: 1
[4] See Acts 9: 1-19
[5] Acts 11: 25-26
[6] See Acts 13: 3
[7] Eugene Peterson, *The Message*, p. 467

6

Perseverance

Just keep going

The sun is just beginning to break through. It whispers its warmth onto his cheek, and welcomes him into the new day. Michel stretches his arms as if in an act of unconscious worship. He grimaces as his shoulders remind him of the constant work that they are being asked to do. He sits up and rolls his neck from side to side trying to ease the stiffness in his muscles and joints. Why do I do this? he thinks to himself.

He remembered the invitation to get involved. It wasn't so much an invitation, as an order. When a man like Julius tells you that he would like something done, then it gets done. 'Michel, I have a job that is just right for you. It is a great honour and will make you famous,' Julius had said in his usual powerful tone. It was not so much his tone as his gaze that almost made Michel a little uneasy. As Julius had gone on to explain the job, Michel had become more and more irritable. 'I am a sculptor, not a painter, I have no interest in this.' Yet, even as he had spoken he knew that Julius had already made up his mind.

Michel stood up slowly and painfully made his way
to the jug and bowl in the corner of the room. He lifted
the jug and bent over the bowl pouring the cold water
down upon his head like some self-anointed king.
Shaking his thick wavy hair dry, he then put on his
clothes and prepared for another day of pain punctuat-
ed by glimpses of delight.

Closing the door behind him he stepped into the bright
Roman sunshine, moving deliberately on towards the
chapel. The heat of the early morning sun warmed his
body, massaging some of the tiredness away filling him
with a renewed sense of hope. He stopped, and looked
around him, soaking up the noises and smells of the early
morning. The city was just coming to life, celebrating the
start of the new day with the normal bustle and action. As
Michel moved on he reflected upon Rome and living
there. He preferred Florence, the town of his family.

Looking around he saw an old man carrying a bundle
of sticks on his back. Michel thought of his father, his
large eyebrows coming together as all his plans for his
son fell apart. His dad, governor of Caprese and born
politician had wanted his son to follow the family
career. However, even his father had to accept that
Michel had the heart of an artist. What else could he be,
coming from Florence? Florence, the city where he had
trained, and spent hours in the studio of the Ghirlandaio
brothers. Florence, the city of Giotto and Masaccio.
Florence, the city with the soul of the artist. How could
he be anything else? However, this was not Florence;
this was Rome. Michel had a job to complete, and he
would do it.

Michel looked up and sighed as his eye scanned the
ceiling. The thought of climbing up the scaffolding one
more time seemed like an ordeal too far. He remembered when he had started this work, almost four years

earlier, marking out the ceilings into panels. He began by sketching out the characters, working from his imagination. His mind was pulled and pushed around as much as his creative talent. Perhaps he should have involved other people in the main body of the work. Yet Michel knew that he couldn't let it go. It was his work and he had invested energy, sweat and eternal tears into this work, and he was not going to give it up. He had started the work and he would finish it.

Climbing up the ladders and planking, Michel eventually got to the top. Again he studied the mass of colour and shape. The beginning of the world, Adam and Eve, the Fall and the flood. Michel was proud of the work that he had done. Not only had he told the stories; he had managed to show that there was an honour and nobility about mankind. Man was a beautiful and wonderful thing, created by an awesome God.

As he lay down again after another long day he whispered a prayer, 'God help me use my gifts to your glory and give me the strength just to carry on.'

Powerpoint – Sometimes it takes real determination just to keep going.

From 1508 to 1512 Michelangelo worked on painting the interior of the Sistine Chapel. He did it almost entirely alone. Michelangelo lay on scaffolding high above the chapel floor. He had to work fast, painting in lots of small strokes on the wet plaster. The ceiling was approximately five thousand yards all around him. It is hard for us to imagine how difficult it must have been just to keep going, for him to get up everyday and persevere, never giving up or throwing in the towel. He worried constantly about his work and the things that could go wrong. It cost him both physically and socially. He must have felt bereft. His determination to complete the work had cost him a great deal. He was physically exhausted, isolated and obsessed by the work to such a degree that his health suffered.

What would have happened if Michelangelo had given up half way into the work? If he had got up one day, feeling the pain in his limbs, and said to himself, 'That's it. I can't take anymore of this. I'm off.' Would he have been recognized as the genius that he was, or would he have been regarded as Michelangelo the might-have-been?

It took great courage and determination to finish the work that he had begun. It involved a lot of sacrifice, but when it was finished, when he stepped down from the scaffolding for the last time and looked up, I bet that he had a great big smile. What a thrill it must have been to see that all his work had made something so breathtakingly beautiful.

It was only because of his determination to get the job finished that millions of people are now touched by his creative genius. It was only because he pulled himself from his bed and up the scaffolding everyday that generations of people are made to stop for a moment and think about less mundane things.

> **Powerpoint** – Without perseverance the genius would never have been revealed.

Rain, what rain?

That same stickability is seen in various stories in the Old Testament. Think of the determination that Moses needed. Imagine having to lead the Israelites for forty years, especially as they often behaved like a bunch of grumps. It must have taken great strength of character to face disappointment and discouragement day after day. His perseverance was a real sign of his faith. Believing that God was gracious and all-powerful meant that Moses could put up with a lot, and still keep going. Sometimes perseverance is about ignoring our feelings and trusting in the sovereign power of God.

Powerpoint – Sometimes when we feel like giving up we need to take our eyes off the situation and onto the sovereignty of God.

My favourite story of keeping going is the story of Noah. It is a story that is quite easy for us to imagine. It is found in the book of Genesis. Let's take a look behind the scenes.

'What is it all about Shem? Why did the old man call a family meeting? It must be something really important.'

Shem's deep dark eyes seemed to sparkle. 'I've no idea. You know what he is like, Ham. He'll let us know in his own time.'

'It's just that he's seemed kind of strange in the last few days. As if he has something on his mind. He hasn't had much to stay. He just says that he needed to spend time with the Lord.'

Shem smiled at his brother before running his hand through his thick black beard. 'You know how dad feels. He has always been a godly man and he can't understand why people act the way they do today. I've tried to tell him that things just change, nothing stays as it was. Every time there is news of another crime it seems to make him sadder.'

Ham had been chewing on his nails as he had listened to his brother. Moving his hands back down onto the plain wooden table he said, 'You know I caught him crying yesterday. He didn't notice that I was watching him. When he realized he quickly wiped his eyes and tried to ignore it, as if it had never happened. I don't think I've ever seen him cry before. As he passed me by he laid his hand on my shoulder and looked into my eyes. All he said was, 'They are breaking God's heart. How long will he stand for it?''

At that point two other people came into the room, stilling the conversation between the brothers. It was obvious, viewing the younger of the two men, that he was related to the two brothers. While being younger, he had the same dark shining eyes and his hair was thick deep and black. He had a confident swagger and a determined stride. He looked at the other two and nodded.

'Hi Japheth', Shem called out.

'Shem, Ham, how are you both?'

For a few minutes the men sat and chatted, asking about one another's families and about news from the town. The other man stood quietly at the door, watching the scene like a portrait painter. While a hint of a smile flitted across his face, it was clear that the man was carrying a heavy burden.

'My sons,' he said in a loud crystal clear voice. He had all their attention. 'As you know I have been gravely concerned by the state of our nation. Wherever you look there is violence and immorality. People ignore and slander the Lord with every breath. It has grieved me, and I have spent many days on my knees before our God. After days of waiting, the Lord has finally revealed his will to me, his servant.'

Noah moved to the head of the table, pulled back a seat and sat down. He looked at them all in turn.

'The Lord is gracious, long suffering and slow to anger but our people have mocked and ridiculed him. His judgement will be upon them.'

Shem looked up from the table and glanced at his brothers. Ham looked up and gave a sad smile before raising his eyebrows in silent resignation.

After a deep breath Noah continued. 'The whole earth is corrupt and the Lord will make an end of all life.'

Noah was speaking quickly, and with a great sense of urgency. After he gave this warning, there was silence in the room. It seemed as if time had stopped as the sons took in what their father had told them. Shem coughed and cleared his throat.

'When is this going to happen father?' he asked quietly.

'I don't know exactly when; it will happen when we have completed our task.'

The other brothers stirred in their seats, unsure how to respond.

'What task?' asked Japheth in a squeaky hesitant tone.

'My son, God has been gracious to us. He has shown his love and has promised to save our families and ourselves, as well as animals and birds of the air.'

'How is he going to do that father? How is God going to save us and destroy everyone else?'

'God is going to bring floodwaters and they will destroy all living things. But we are not to worry, for God will protect us.'

Japheth looked up, confused and uncertain. 'So, let me get this right father. God is going to send a huge flood and everything will be destroyed except us. We'll be saved and we have an important task to do. Is that right?' he said, desperately trying to keep the incredulity from his voice.

Ham jumped in with renewed confidence, 'So dad, what is this great task that we are to complete?'

'We are to build an ark. It will take a lot of work. It is to be our refuge. It will be like a huge security chest in which we will go when the flood starts.'

'When you say huge, just how big are we talking about father?' asked Shem, feeling that he had to say something.

Noah looked at them. 'It will take a lot of work. It is to be 450 feet long, 75 feet wide and 45 feet high. It will have three sets of decks and the whole thing will be covered in pitch.'

The brothers were totally silent, unable to find any words to express how they felt. They don't live anywhere near the sea. They have no experience of shipbuilding, and they wonder whether their dad has been out in the sun too long.

Shem speaks up for them all. 'Look dad, we know nothing about these things. How is this going to happen?'

Noah smiled. 'My sons when you have lived as long as I have, you learn one thing. With God all things are possible. God is able.'

Can you imagine what it must have been like for that family as the ark began to take shape and people walked by? It must have been a great conversation starter. I wonder how many times Noah and his family were the butt of jokes. It must have been really hard to keep working when there were no visible signs that what you were doing would make any difference. Day after day, getting the wood, putting it together, keeping the shape and knowing that you were the centre of every joke from every smart guy within your society.

It says a lot about Noah and his relationship with God, the fact that he kept going, and that he and his family persevered.

> **Powerpoint** – It can be hard to keep going when there are no visible signs that what we are doing is making any difference.

M and M

Hearing parents talk about when their children were learning to walk reminded me that perseverance is as a quality of spiritual life. The picture came up again and again of the small child taking those first few steps, with the encouragement of the parent. Faltering and uncertain yet groundbreaking steps are taken. The family treat these steps as being as significant as those of Edmund Hillary when he reached the summit of Everest. After the child has taken these momentous advances they fall over, and look around totally bewildered. Then the toddler pushes themselves up in a very unflattering way and tries again. They walk and fall over and over again. Yet for all the bumps and struggles they never get to the place where they give up. There is not a time when the toddler decides that they don't want to walk; that they will spend their entire life simply crawling around.

The desire to keep trying is found in the lives of all children. When they face a setback they try again undeterred. One of my children is now thirteen years old. At the moment he has a lot of bruises on his shins, and one or two on his wrist. When you ask him about how he got them, he will explain that he has been on his skateboard. Each bruise signals another attempt at perfecting a new move.

'This happened when I tried an "Olly". That one was when I tried a heel flip.'

They are mentioned like medals in a campaign. It has never entered his mind to give up. To get better you have to take the knocks and keep going. We will never get better at something if we give up at the first sign of difficulty.

> **Powerpoint** – There is no growth without taking the knocks. The secret is getting up and keeping going.

This idea of keeping going, taking time and sticking at things is not popular in our culture. Let me give you three illustrations about our instant culture.

Media

Have you ever tried to sit down and watch a whole programme on television with your family? Especially if the programme you are watching happens to be on satellite TV. One minute you are watching a smiling man dancing with an elephant encouraging you to check your finances then suddenly it is Hercule Poirot. From one image to another you are left spinning, as if you had been on a waltzer ride at the carnival.

Turning to look around the room you see a member of the family, remote control in hand. Just as you are about to make a comment, the channel is changed again and the original show is just coming back on screen. Looking at the child, they are putting down the remote like a gunfighter at the OK Corral. The idea of just waiting for the story to start again was not an option. In the thirty seconds there was the chance to check out other things. The same thing happens with music. Instead of listening all the way through an album, we go track by track until we find something that suits the mood. Listening all the way through, just waiting until the next track, sticking with it – certainly not.

Mail

Do you remember what it was like to get a letter? A real letter, not a circular nor a bill, but getting a note from someone who had sat down and taken the time to put some of their thoughts on paper. Not only that, but the person then took the time to remember your address, get an envelope, find a stamp and then post the letter to you. There was something nice about receiving a letter from someone who was genuinely interested. To read the note through a couple of times and visualize the sender. Mulling over what information was helpful or funny, what stories to pass on and what gossip to share. To have time to stop, reflect and answer.

Now I live by e-mail. The good thing is that I get information rapidly; the bad thing is that people want a response just as rapidly. The process of thinking about the person and what to say to them is speeded up. It is amazing to think that I can make plans and discuss arrangements about speaking in a church in America, and have replies within an hour. The time to consider and picture has been removed. So too has the discipline of waiting; the wonder of whether the person has replied, and what they have thought of your response to them. Holding on in the hope that they would write back, that you matter enough to them for them to take time to reply. All that has gone as I click on my internet server, and the voice of a well-known American actress and celebrity says to me, 'You've got mail.'

Microwave

I'd got about twenty minutes for lunch. I'd been at a planning meeting in the morning and I was heading for the secondary school in the afternoon. I rushed in, threw down my briefcase and headed into the kitchen. In a past generation I would have had to wait for the soup to heat up on the stove. Not anymore. I rush towards the microwave, open it up then turn to the fridge, pick up a pre-packed burger then ram it into the machine and switch it on for one minute. Getting a can of Coke from the cupboard, I pour it in a glass full of ice. After taking just a sip the bell rings to let me know lunch is served. It's not that tasty or nutritious, but it is quick. The microwave is a marvellous invention: I don't need to bother with food preparation, recipes or cooking time. The most that I am stretched to is to switch the timer to the appropriate level.

All of the things that I have mentioned are now part of most of our lives. There is nothing wrong with any of them. Indeed they can give us more choice and freedom. However, the problem comes when this 'instant' culture impacts our ministry as part of the people of God. I am not talking about the pace of life or the pressure of busyness that we all face. I have mentioned these things before.[1] Here I am trying to highlight our need for instant gratification. We want things to happen now. It is that desire for the instant that can become a danger, particularly when that mind-set drives our spiritual life. When our lives become driven by the need to reap rather than sow, when we judge things by the now rather than the hereafter and when we have to know everything quickly rather than understand in part.

Powerpoint – We need to look beyond the instant, gaining an eternal perspective.

This is seen in many churches that find it increasingly difficult to get workers involved in things that will take the long haul.

While churches can get people to support an outreach evening or a fun day, it is becoming harder to get people to commit to helping with long-term ministry. Although this may be down to work and pace of life, I don't think that is the main factor. The main factor is instant culture beginning to invade the way in which we view our whole life, including church.

Diving for pennies

The London Marathon is a wonderful event. As the television cameras sweep the starting line we are given a glimpse of the diversity of the world: serious athletes ready to challenge one another on to ever-faster times, and others facing their own private challenges. Many run to raise funds for charity, and some wear the most wonderful costumes. They bring a joy to the event and to life. For a few seconds we are able to wonder at the human spirit and at the compassion of people. To see people giving of themselves, going through the wall of tiredness and persevering to raise money for a worthy cause is a great thing. I have always been interested in the really unusual stories surrounding the marathon.

Last year one particular story caught my attention. It was about the man who ran the whole of the London Marathon wearing a full diving suit. His name was Lloyd Scott and he came from Essex . He ran 26 miles in a 130lb diving suit. He was running for a children's cancer charity and raised thousands of pounds. What really interested me was the time that it took to complete the race. He started on the Sunday morning and finished at

6.17pm on the Friday. It took 128 hours 29 minutes and 46 seconds.

I wonder how many times Lloyd felt like giving up. He started the challenge always knowing that he was never going to be near the front. Indeed most people were back at work basking in their triumph while he was still plodding away. Yet he just kept going. Partly, that must have been due to the character of the man; partly it must have been because of the reason he was running it. He was able to carry on because of the support he got from others. It was the cheers along the way that reminded him that he was not forgotten. The cars honking horns, and the passers-by cheering gave him renewed energy.

It was a remarkable effort. There are spiritual lessons to be learned for us here. In order to persevere, we need to have the character, and we also need to remember how important the cause is to which we have been called. However, perhaps the greatest incentive to persevere is to know that others are cheering us on. It is great to know that others care and that they are with us on the journey of faith.

Powerpoint – To persevere we need to share the journey with others.

When we think of the apostle Paul's famous words on running the race[2] it might be helpful to think of some of the stories surrounding marathon-running. To think of the struggle, the pain, but also the joy of reaching the finishing line. For Christians the great encouragement is that there are spiritual brothers and sisters praying and caring for us. But the greater encouragement comes from knowing that Jesus ran the race before us and now travels the race with us: preparing the best route, pointing out the potholes and picking us up as we trip and stumble. Then when we feel as though we can't go any further, his voice calls to us in tones of compassion and love, reminding us of that glorious finishing line. It is important for us to remember that our salvation was made possible because Jesus saw the thing through to the end.

Getting the job done

A crunch time for Jesus is found towards the end of Luke 9.[3] Here he begins a journey towards Jerusalem. In fact Luke tells us that Jesus resolutely set out for Jerusalem. This could be translated to mean that he set his face to go to Jerusalem. It portrays a conscious strengthening of heart and concentration of mind, and a stiffening of the will. *The Message* says 'he gathered up his courage and steeled himself for the journey.'[4] It can't have been easy to make a journey, knowing that it would be your last, and the encounters in the next few verses underline just how difficult it must have been.

First Jesus sends messengers to a village in Samaria to prepare a place of rest from the journey for him (verse 52). However, the villagers don't want him there. It must have saddened Jesus to know this. Consider all the times that Jesus had given himself to people. There must have been many moments when he was exhausted, and yet he continued to reach out in love.

When the disciples hear about the reaction of the villagers, James and John offer to call down fire from heaven to destroy them. After all that time with Jesus – after seeing how he had dealt with and loved his enemies, they want to destroy the village! I picture Jesus putting his head in his hands, then rubbing tired eyes and wondering if his disciples will ever really get it.

How could they come up with an idea like that? All we are told is that Jesus rebuked them (verse 55). It must have been so discouraging to have to deal with responses like that from those closest to him. Just when he was preparing himself for what lay ahead, he is faced with a lack of openness in the village and a totally inappropriate response from James and John.

If this were not bad enough, there are the encounters with people who want a low-cost discipleship. There are three exchanges, and in each Jesus underlines the fact that following him involves radical commitment. In the first, a man tells Jesus that he would be willing to follow him anywhere. Jesus makes it clear to the man that to follow is to wave goodbye to any guarantee of material security. To follow would be to give over your life. Secondly, a man wants to come and follow when he has dealt with important domestic issues. While we may think that the man's plea seems reasonable, it gives Jesus the chance to underline once again the radical nature of discipleship. Old order responsibilities, although important, don't compare with the call to the new order brought through Jesus. The third person in these encounters wants to follow Jesus, but again has family ties that he wants to wrap up before following Jesus. In reply to this Jesus makes this radical statement, 'No one who puts his hand to the plough and looks back is fit for the service in the kingdom of God.' (verse 62)

Jesus was mirroring that statement in his own life. What a time for him. He has to steal himself and set off towards Jerusalem. Within a short space of doing so, he is rejected by a village, misunderstood by disciples and has to spell out again what true discipleship is. All this was faced by the one who refused to reject people, whatever their track record. He never misunderstood the needs of others and he took up his own cross daily, showing exactly what discipleship entailed. Despite all that, Jesus kept going, running the race, no matter the cost.

It may be that you have fallen while running the road of faith. Allow him to lift you up again. Perhaps, you are about to give up, feeling it is no longer worth it. You have used up the energy that you had, and now there is only an empty shell. Picture the finishing line and the one who runs the race with you. Don't give up: persevere, keep going. This part may have gruelling, but there is a slight descent, with a gentle breeze.

Reflection

'With your help I can advance against a troop; with my God I can scale a wall' (Ps. 18: 29)

I have never been good at climbing. It has something to do with co-ordination. My hands and feet never quite work together as I want them to. Yet now would be a good time to learn. There is a wall right here before me. It seems massive, and there doesn't appear to be a way round it. It seems like I will just have to climb over it. If I am going to keep up with you then I will have to get over this huge barrier in my way.

This is not the first wall that I have had to get over and it probably won't be the last. All the others have been a real struggle but I have always managed to get over. There were times when I slipped and almost feel. Each time it was just thinking about the next move. Just keep going.

Lord, no matter what the wall is, I can climb it; if you give me a hitch-up I know that I can get there.

Questions

1. If you feel like giving up, stop and think about the one who travels with you.
2. Is it possible for you to encourage others who are finding the journey of faith difficult? How might you achieve this?

Prayer

Lord, there are times when I feel breathless.
I seem to be running up a hill all the time.
The easiest thing to do would be to give up.
At these times Lord make me more aware of your presence.
Help me to listen to your promptings.
Keep the finishing line ever before me.
And I thank you Lord for the people whom you send to cheer me on.
Amen.

---

[1] See chapter one
[2] See Philippians 3: 12
[3] See Luke 9: 51-56
[4] Eugene Peterson, *The Message*, p. 170

7

Tears

Crying over you – open my heart Lord

We all have days that stay in our minds forever: things that happen that imprint on our hearts permanently. Sometimes in quiet moments we are surprised by a sudden memory that makes us shudder or laugh. The day that I am about to describe was such a day.

There was a growing excitement amongst us. Jesus was moving with even greater passion and pace than he had before. He had been teaching us about the Kingdom of God. Now we were heading back towards Jerusalem. Jesus had met with a tax collector called Zacchaeus. He was a short, stocky man with hard eyes and a reputation for being heartless. However, when he encountered Jesus, he was able to show Zacchaeus the power of the love of God, and the need for change in his life. Zacchaeus heard the message with openness and there was a real change in the heart of the man. So much so that he was willing to give to the poor and to repay those that he had cheated.

After this encounter, Jesus told a parable. I was getting more used to parables now; at first I was totally lost.

Sometimes when Jesus talked it was like a big dark rain cloud surrounded me. I used to think that I must be the most stupid, thick, ignorant disciple that any master could have. It was a great relief to find that most of the others didn't understand either. Yet Jesus was always patient with us. I don't know why. I think if I had been in his shoes I would have got rid of us all and started again. But that would just not be the Jesus way. No matter what we said, there was never a time when we felt that Jesus was giving up on us. Now, after all the time spent with him, I felt that I had a chance of understanding what he was going to say. I also knew that if I didn't understand then I could wait for a quiet moment to ask him.

Powerpoint – Don't give up. There is never a time when God gives up on you.

Jesus' story was about a man who was going to be king.[1] The man went on a journey, but before he went, he called ten servants to be brought to his private chambers. The chambers were beautiful, highlighting the man's wealth. It was full of exquisite things from far and wide. Normally the servants did not see this chamber, and as they stood outside they wondered why they had been called. What had they done? The servants ranged from young to old and worked in different parts of the house and wider estate. One or two of the juniors were so nervous that their stomachs were rumbling loudly. It sounded like a band of musicians all starting up at once.

After a few minutes, which seemed like hours, the servants were called into the presence of the master. They all wondered what the master might say to them. It was a remarkable request. So strange that, at first, many of the servants could not believe what they were being told. The master looked at each one in turn, his eyes burning into theirs, searching for something that only he knew.

'I have a very important job for you to do,' he said.

He then took ten small bags and gave one to each of the servants. He took each one by the hand and placed the bag in the centre of their palm. When he got to the end of the line of servants the master walked slowly back to the centre of the group. Every eye was upon him, wondering what was going to happen next. The whole scene was very weird; each servant holding a bag, its contents unknown, waiting to find out what would happen next.

His voice was clear and proud, and as he spoke, it seemed as if a burden was being lifted from the servants' shoulders.

'I am going on a journey. You do not need to know where or for how long. While I am away, I have a very important task for each one of you.

'In each bag there is more money than any of you have ever seen before. Each bag holds a mina – more than three month's wages. You may wonder why I have given it to you. You may think that I have gone mad. You may be silly enough to think that this is your lucky day.' He looked at them and a faint smile flitted across his lips. 'I can assure you that none of these things are true.'

He spoke more sternly, reminding the servants, by his tone, who he was.

'When I return I shall be king. However, while I am away I want you to make my money grow. I want to hear of profits growing and interest accruing. This is a great chance for you. Of all the people I could have chosen, I have chosen you, and I am entrusting you with some of my wealth. It is there in your hands.'

Several servants glanced furtively at the bags in their hand; the rest kept staring intently at the floor.

He ran his hand through his dark, long hair. He stood in silence, twisting the large gold ring on the middle finger of his right hand. 'What a privilege you have to be given some of the master's riches. The question is what will you do with them? As soon as I come back, I will demand an account of what you have done with the things that I have given you.'

> **Powerpoint** – God has gifted you with so many of his riches.

Time past and the master eventually came back to his estate. He had many things to do when he came home. There were ceremonial duties, social occasions and vital matters of state. He seemed to be permanently busy. Being king involved a lot of his time and energy. However, he never forgot his servants or the money that had been entrusted to them.

It was early in the morning and the sun had already risen. The servants were called from their duties and lined up in the courtyard. They stood in silence, knowing that the time of reckoning was at hand. They stood waiting for some time, each second adding to the tension.

At last they were marched into the chamber and there, sitting on a large wooden chair beautifully carved with images of birds and flowers on its back, was the king. His elbows rested on an equally ornate table. He stood up, came around to the front of the table and leaned against it. He had the look of a contented man. As he gazed at the servants he played with the gold ring. He took several minutes to weigh up what he wanted to say.

'Before I left I gave each one of you an important task to do. Your job was a simple one: use what you were given to make more. Now I have returned and I am anxious to see what you have done with what you were given.'

The king then stretched out his hand and pointed with his long manicured finger at the servant who stood closest to him. 'Well, what did you do with what I gave you?'

The servant lifted his gaze from the floor and looked at the master. He was extremely nervous and when he spoke his voice was little more than a whisper.

'Master, the money that you gave me has earned ten more.'

With that he handed the bag he was originally given back to the master. The bag was brimming with coins. The master weighed the bag in his hand and a huge grin spread across his face. He stepped forward and patted the servant on the shoulder.

'Well done, well done,' he said enthusiastically. 'You have been faithful in this small task, I now have a bigger job for you to do. As you have shown yourself to be trustworthy, I want you to take charge of ten cities within my kingdom.'

The servants looked in disbelief, one or two of the others gasped, unable to control themselves. What a responsibility and privilege for the servant. His trustworthiness and the generosity of his master meant that his life would never be the same again.

It was a few moments before the servants remembered where they were and order descended again. Then the king thrust out his finger like an arrow targeting another servant. The servant was slightly older than the others. His hair was greying at the sides and he had a rounding of the shoulders from years of heavy carrying. He looked scared.

'Step forward.'

The servant shuffled ahead two steps, his head bowed. 'Tell me, what did you do with what you have been given?' asked the king.

'Master,' replied the servant, 'the mina you gave to me has gained five more. You gave me one now I can return six.'

The servant did not know where he had found the courage to speak. In all his years of service he had never spoken more than a few words to the master.

Nodding, the master gripped the hand of the servant, 'I knew I was right. Well done, you will take charge of five cities. You have proven yourself.'

Then the master looked again at the line of servants. This time he inclined his head towards the servant who was last in the line. The servant took a step forward and handed the master the bag. It was much lighter than the others he had received. He opened the bag, pulling apart the ties. With a dramatic sweep the master then tipped the contents out into his left hand. Instead of coins there was a torn piece of cloth. Undoing the cloth he found one mina – the same coin that the master had given the servant before the master had taken his journey.

'What is the meaning of this?' barked the king. 'Well, explain yourself.'

'Master, I was scared of you. I didn't want to lose it, so I kept it safely, awaiting your return. Everybody knows that you are a hard man and so...'

The king interrupted the servant with a raised hand and a look that signalled he didn't want to hear anymore.

'You did nothing with what I gave you. Even though you knew that I would come back and demand an account.

'You did not even have the sense to put it on deposit and gain some interest. Was it fear, lack of trustworthiness or laziness that prevented you from doing anything?'

With that he took the mina and gave it to the one who had made the ten.

Jesus finished the story with the words, 'I tell you that to everyone who has, more will be given but as for the ones who have nothing even what he has will be taken away from him.'

Powerpoint – What are we doing with the gifts God has given us?

I pondered these words over and over again as we headed towards Jerusalem. Eventually we reached the hill that was called the 'Mount of Olives'.

I was still lost in thought when Jesus turned to face us. He stopped and sat on a rock and gazed into space. There were times when it was impossible for us to know what was going through Jesus' mind. I felt that these times were happening more frequently now.

'Two of you are to go into the village and when you get there you will find a colt tied up. It has never been ridden before. Untie it and bring it back here,' Jesus said.

Another disciple and myself got up from where we were sitting and started to move off.

'If anyone asks you why you are untying it, just tell him that the Lords needs it!' he shouted after us.

We found the colt exactly as he said we would, untied it and started to lead it back to where Jesus and the rest of the disciples were resting.[2] Just after we had untied it two men approached us. One was a large man, balding and out of breath in the heat of the day. His face was red, and he was using a large cloth to wipe the sweat from his eyes. The other was younger and a little smaller. The large man looked at us with suspicion in his eyes.

'Why are you untying the colt?' He spoke the words as if he were about to accuse us of stealing.

We looked at one another and then remembered what Jesus had said: 'The Lord needs it.'

The two men began to smile, and then they laughed, as if something amazing was taking place. The younger man spoke. 'Take the colt and go in peace.'

I was completely confused. I mean it was a nice colt and it was good of them to give it to us. However, I just couldn't understand their reaction. Being confused is not something that I am completely unfamiliar with though.

As we arrived back, I was struck straight away by the noise and the din of children chattering with excitement. Jesus was smiling in that humble, compassionate way that said to each person that they had a place, that there was room for them, no matter who they were. Today, as he rode on the colt he made me think of a king coming home from a war, riding at the front of a triumphal procession. Some children on the shoulders of adults yelled with excitement.

Others must have had similar feelings to my own, for as he was moving along, people would step forward and lay cloaks down on the road. It looked like a multi-coloured carpet – a mosaic of giving, revealing how Jesus had touched the hearts of those gathered.

Powerpoint – Let your praise like petals fall at the feet of Jesus as you journey with him.

As we descended the Mount of Olives more disciples joined us. They were laughing and praising God,

celebrating the good things that God had done in send-
ing his anointed one to us. Some shouted words from
the psalms, others from the prophets. There was a real
buzz about the place. It felt wonderful to be alive and to
be part of this day. Suddenly the atmosphere changed.
As if from nowhere the sky filled with a dark cloud.
Looking back now I can say that it was the first chill of
the gathering storm.

It began with some Pharisees who had been in the
crowd of onlookers. What they saw did not bring forth
praise from their lips, but accusation. Pushing through
the crowd they had approached Jesus.

'Teacher, rebuke your disciples.'

A look of sadness creased Jesus' face. When he spoke
it was with a low quiet voice. He looked into their eyes,
as if he were searching their very souls. Then he slowly
shook his head.

'I tell you the truth,' he replied, 'if they kept quiet, the
stones will cry out.' He nodded and the colt moved on,
leaving them in the dust of the road.

With these words Jesus headed on his journey
towards Jerusalem. While the praise continued for a little while, the atmosphere was broken. Jesus got off the
colt and stood on his own, a little apart from the rest of
the group. We were still in good spirits, encouraging
one another with stories of the crowds, the laughter
and the fun of the day. While the Pharisees had damp-
ened our day, we still marvelled at it. God was doing
exciting things. Was this the start of some monumental
event?

I moved away from the others. Perhaps this would be
a good time to ask about the parable of the ten minas
that he had recently told us. I approached Jesus quietly,
stepping gently to his side. He didn't move. His breath-
ing was shallow and his shoulders were moving gently

up and down. As I gazed at his face, large tears were cascading down his cheeks. I didn't know what to do. Any comments I made would have seemed so out of place. I wanted to touch him; to reassure him things couldn't be that bad. Surely, the day had been a good one. Yet somehow my courage deserted me in the face of this private grief. As I stepped gently away I heard him whisper between sobs. Fixing his gaze on the city he said: 'If you, even you, had only known on this day what would bring you peace.'

* * *

It is astonishing to think that at this time in Jesus' life, his tears were not for himself. There is no tinge of self-pitying in Jesus' character, nor does he weep for the disciples and all that awaits them, the situations that they would face and the joys and trials ahead. Jesus weeps for the city. Jerusalem with all its history and all its blessing. Yet, as Jesus gazes at it through moist eyes, he sees missed opportunity. He knows that the people race around ignoring the great chance that was in their midst. Touchable grace was on their doorstep and they slammed the door shut.

Powerpoint – Touchable grace is at the door of your life. Don't slam shut the door.

A city lost and scarred by missed opportunity touched Jesus. Time and again we are reminded in the gospels that Jesus was moved with compassion.[3] Here his compassion and the frustration of rejected compassion are shaken together in the mixer of his heart and poured out like rivers on his face.

Family time

Jesus also shed tears for those close to him. Jesus knew a family of a brother and two sisters. Their names were Lazarus, Martha and Mary, and the gospels tell us that Jesus loved them. John relates the story of Lazarus' illness, death and the way in which Jesus brought him back to life.[4] It is a powerful incident highlighting tragedy, loss, love and hope. Most wonderfully it is a time when Jesus reveals who he is so that his friends may have their faith strengthened and their hope renewed.

Rather than rushing straight away when Jesus is told about Lazarus' illness, he waited two days. Imagine the sisters desperately hoping that Jesus would come, nervous flustered and exhausted, praying that the illness would not be fatal. If Jesus would just get there then Lazarus could be healed and everything would be all right. However, Jesus doesn't work to other people's timescales, and he didn't then. Jesus was the only one who could see the whole picture.

Powerpoint – Only Jesus can see the whole picture of our lives.

Eventually Jesus makes his way to the home of Lazarus. Lazarus has now been dead for several days. There are mourners and family there, united in grief. Word arrives that Jesus is nearby. What would be the reaction of those lost in sorrow? How would they cope with the apparent late arrival of their friend?

Martha leaves the house and goes to meet Jesus, her body exhausted and her eyes tired and red from too little sleep and too many tears. When she looks at Jesus there is no bitterness or criticism but a statement of faith: 'I know that even now God will give you whatever you ask.'

Jesus said to her, 'Your brother will rise again.'

Martha answered, 'I know that he will rise again in the resurrection on the last day.'

Jesus said to her, 'I am the resurrection and the life. He who believes in me will live, even though he dies, and whoever lives and believes in me will never die. Do you believe this?'

It is hard for us to do justice to the tension of that moment. We are too detached by time and circumstance. But try to imagine Martha. Her family is being torn to shreds. The brother she loves is dead and in his tomb, the mourners are still at the house. The one that you had asked to come quickly turns up late, and then makes this amazing, fantastic, wonderful claim.

'Yes Lord,' she told him, 'I believe that you are the Christ, the Son of God, who has come into the world.'

What a monumental response! She is trusting Jesus with her past, present and future. Even when her circumstances are at an all time low, she is able to take Jesus at his word and trust him.

After their conversation Martha hurries back to the house to get Mary. We are not told why Mary did not come with Martha originally. Perhaps she was too grief-stricken to leave the house. Maybe she felt a responsibility to the other mourners and did not want to leave them. Could there have been a tension in her mind and heart about meeting Jesus again? Whatever the reason, things changed as soon as Martha told her that Jesus was asking for her.

As soon as Mary realized that Jesus' concern for her had not changed she rushed to him. She sees him in the distance and runs to him. When she gets close to him she is overcome. The tensions of the past few days, the compassion of Jesus, the presence of all the other mourners all crash upon her heart. She falls to her knees at Jesus' feet. Through the anguish and the tears she looks up at him.

'Lord if you had been here, my brother would not have died.'

Jesus looked into her eyes and felt her pain and sorrow. Then slowly glancing at the mourners who surrounded her, he saw the hurts that they were all carrying. It was impossible for Jesus to keep all this at arm's length. His love was visible, touchable and vulnerable. It is love that refuses to be chained, or given by degree. As he witnessed their pain, he was deeply moved in spirit and troubled. He felt their loss deeply. More than that he knew what sin and separation from God had led to. Here, in this family whom he loved, was an image of the pain that life and death brought to every person.

As Jesus looked upon this scene he wept. He wept for them, he wept for the world. He wept because he was moved by the plight of the human condition. A condition that he would change forever.

John continues the story, detailing how Jesus prayed to his father and then raised Lazarus from the dead, that act being a visual demonstration of the claim he made to being the 'resurrection and the life'.

However, it was not his power that is of most interest to us but his tears. Jesus allowed events and people to touch his heart. He was always ready to draw near to those who experienced loss. He did not skip round people in their need, offering a trite cliché of sympathy before moving on to more important matters. Instead, his love drew him to hurting people and they moved him.

When my niece, Karen, was young she learned a song at the Brownies:

'Good morning friend Brownie,
How are you this morning?
We dance in a circle and
Bow and pass on.'[5]

It is a nice little verse, but it is not the Jesus way. Unlike many of us he did not just say good morning, ask how you are, and pass on.

Powerpoint – Jesus doesn't address us in trite clichés, but in loving truth.

Weeping before the Lord

Anyone who has spent much time with children will know that they cry for a whole host of different reasons. Sometimes they cry out of need. If the baby is hungry they cry for food. If it is thirsty they cry for drink. Children also cry if they are uncertain or unsure. Remember that heart-rending cry as you left your baby for the first time to go out for a night together? Then there are the tears of anger, frustration and confusion.

To reflect upon this list we might think that children spend all their time crying. Of course this is not the case – the tears are the break in the norm, which alert others to a situation that the child is in.

In the Bible we find people weeping for many of the same reasons. Some are brought low because of their personal situation. Esau, Jacob, Job, David and Ruth are all examples of people who wept bitter tears at times when their lives were in turmoil and things were not going quite the way that they planned.

Powerpoint – Scripture has a litany of tears, perhaps it is a list of honour.

Others have wept over the state of the people of God and the honour that was due to God's name. Think of Nehemiah. Into his house comes Hanani, a brother with some news.[6] The news is about those of his people who had survived the exile and were now back in Jerusalem. Nehemiah had hoped that the walls of Jerusalem would have been rebuilt, bringing security and also reminding others of the glory of God.

The news that Nehemiah gets is awful. The people are in disgrace, they are arguing with each other and they have done nothing about the walls and gates of the city. Nehemiah tells us his response to this news: 'When I heard these things I sat down and wept. For some days I mourned and fasted and prayed before the God of Heaven.'[7]

He was devastated by the news. What a witness this was, a divided people and a decayed building. Nehemiah cared so much about the glory of God that he was heart-broken by what he heard. His sorrow led him to cry out to the Lord.

Powerpoint – In the face of bad news Nehemiah shed tears for God's glory, not for himself.

Another area of life that has led people to tears in the Bible is the relationship between the individual and God. The psalms are filled with questions about the world, the individual and God. In Psalm 35 we have a picture of someone who is trying to reconcile difficulty in his life with what God is doing in the midst of it. The psalmist writes in verse 14:

'When my prayers returned to me unanswered, I went about mourning, as though for my friend or brother. I bowed my head in grief as though weeping for my mother.'

In verse 22 he goes on to write,

'O LORD you have seen this, be not silent, do not be far from me O LORD'.

There is anguish here and a need for the knowledge of the closeness of the Lord. The writer weeps, longing for the presence of God, and these themes are echoed in many of the psalms.

In Scripture people are brought to their knees before the Lord for various reasons. Some are moved because they have a passion for the glory of God and long to see this name praised. Others cry out because they are going through times of darkness and pain. They are facing issues within life that they can no longer cope with. This sense of hopelessness leads to a crying out. There are also those who long for a deeper knowledge of the presence of God. They ache for that deep intimate fellowship with the living God.

If Jesus wept and many others in Scripture wept why do I find it difficult to be moved by spiritual things? Surely part of our spiritual growth will mean that there will be times when both as individuals and as a church we learn to weep before the Lord.

A pneumatic drill for a wall around the heart

I cry quite a lot. Of course I try not to let anyone see. Sitting in a quiet place listening to some piece of music can bring tears. Some films can also touch me. I really like *Casablanca* and have watched it on countless occasions. I know most of the script off by heart, and there are no surprises left for me. However, it still has that ability to move me. The wind is blowing and a storm is brewing, the skies are dark and there is a sense of unresolved tension in the air. There stands Humphrey Bogart, tough yet vulnerable as only he can be. His raincoat wrapped around him, the collar up against the cold.

He looks at the beautiful Ingrid Bergman and her husband Paul Henreid. Then he takes from his coat pocket the papers that they will need to leave the country and head for freedom. He sacrifices love and his own personal happiness for the greater good. He watches as the couple head away towards the plane and a new life. I am not sure why I find this movie so memorable. It is more than just the acting and direction. Perhaps it is the theme: sacrifice, love and the greatest good. There is something noble and 'old world' about it. Whatever it is, I always find it moving.

I can cry at a piece of music, films and other art, and yet I don't often weep about the things that really matter. I wonder if you are the same. It seems to me that there are things that should make us cry before God. There are areas of life that should force us to our knees in passionate sharing of who we are with our God. Let me give you some examples of the sort of things I mean.

As a young Christian I read a lot about the life of Robert Murray M'Cheyne. He was a minister in the Church of Scotland who was involved in a time of revival in Dundee during the early 1800s. His life was marked by a desire for personal holiness and a closeness to God. In his diary entry for 1 March 1835 he writes, 'What change is there in the heart! Wild, earthly affections there are here: strong, coarse passions; bands both of iron and silk. But I thank thee O my God, that they make me cry, 'O wretched man!'[8] Again in 6 March 1836 he writes after preaching: 'Preacher with some tenderness of heart. O why should I not weep, as Jesus did over Jerusalem?'[9]

This sense of sorrow at sin and a desire to know the love of Jesus more and more in his life marked M'Cheyne out as a person of God. God used him in amazing ways in the lives of many. Perhaps there are times when the desire for personal holiness should lead us to cry before God that the presence of the Lord might cleanse and renew us. I know that M'Cheyne lived in a different era and in a different context. However, the need for closeness to God should evoke within us both a cry for mercy and a longing deep within our souls.

Powerpoint – How much longing in our hearts is there for God?

Another area that should touch our hearts is the state of the church in the western world. Let me say that I think that God is doing many wonderful things in the church. There are a lot of creative things happening and people serving God with great faithfulness and love. However, we are living in a time of uncertainty and decline. The place of the church in our society has moved from the centre much nearer to the margins. The voice of Christian people no longer carries the influence that it once did. We are in a time of change, which sometimes makes us uncomfortable and frightened. What is God doing? What will the church look like in the next few years? For some of us these are exciting questions. However, for all of us these should be questions that lead us to pray with great passion that the Lord might direct his people and pour out the Holy Spirit. If ever there was a time in the history of the church that should bring us to tears, then it is now.

In our church we have used the book *Bound to be Free* from time to time.[10] It is a book of 365 daily readings and prayers contributed by those who are part of the suffering church. When we have used these prayers, they have never failed to touch hearts. Surely the trials of the wider church should help us to direct our thoughts and prayers with renewed vigour. Part of our calling is to allow our tears to flow with those who are in distress and those who are facing the wrath of the world for the sake of the Kingdom of God.

Powerpoint – How much time do we spend thinking about our brothers and sisters in the suffering church?

When we take time to stop and consider the state of the church and the plight of others, we are challenged to care as Jesus cares. The weight on our hearts should make us weep before the Lord and plead for an outpouring of love and mercy.

Yet much of our individual Christian lives and corporate church life is not marked by such passion. Perhaps we have become hardened to the things that are happening around us. There are so many scenes of sorrow and heartache on our television that it is easy to become immune to need. There are scenes that flash on to our screens that no longer move us. It is easy to become desensitized to the hurts in the world.

Powerpoint – Is the media's reaction to the sorrows of the world making us more callous?

It is not easy to allow others to see our pain. Becoming vulnerable and open both to God and to others takes a lot of courage and love. This is especially so if we have been hurt by others in the past. If we have sought to love with our whole being, sharing who we are at a deep level, and then had this thrown back in our faces, we put on the defensive. When we have been let down then we are much more reluctant to open our hearts again.

This attitude is perfectly understandable but can hinder our walk with God. Jesus calls us into a deep and trusting relationship. A relationship marked by ever growing intimacy and dependence. This requires vulnerability and honesty. It involves allowing God access to the whole of our lives. This closeness involves integrity on our part. We have to learn to be who we really are before God. We must allow God into our pain and our joys, letting him bring healing and hope into our lives.

Think again of Jesus. There were many times when his love was rejected. He often found people trying to catch him out and turn his words against him. He was pure and perfect and yet he was rejected by those he tried to help. How painful that must have been. I have often wondered how many tears of disappointment Jesus shed in his quiet times with his father. Yet there was never a time when Jesus kept his distance. Never a time when his heart became hardened. The one who calls us to intimacy is the one who knows all about hurt and letdown.

Powerpoint – The one who calls us to vulnerability knows all about sorrow and letdown.

To reach closeness with Jesus there will be times when we allow God into the deepest recesses of our hearts. He is the faithful one, the one whom we can give the whole of our lives to. While this may not be easy for us to do, it is part of growing closer to God. Ultimately our tears will merge with his and eventually become tears of joy.

The vulnerable community

What a miracle the church is. God brings together a whole bunch of people with different backgrounds, intellects and gifts and makes them into one community. It is not a perfect community, but it should be growing. Growing particularly in love for God, one another and the wider world. Part of that growth should be that we can come into this fellowship as we are, without having to wear spiritual masks to cover up our own doubts and concerns.

I remember a weekly church prayer meeting that I used to attend when I was a young Christian. Every week we would have a list of things to pray for: other churches, people in hospital and missionaries. There were a lot of caring faithful folk who attended regularly and prayed consistently for the work of God. However, I remember from time to time wondering if I was the only person who ever had big questions and ever longed for a deeper walk with the Lord. I felt that this could not be the case, but there was little personal reflection and little sharing about our journey of faith. It was not a time, or perhaps place, for people to either laugh or cry. I don't believe that this is what God envisaged in a growing community of believing people. The church should be a community that is a healing place for every member.

> **Powerpoint** – The community of Christ should be a people of vulnerability and healing.

There are times when the only honest response that we can make is to weep. It is in these times that we are drawn into a deeper relationship of love, knowing the gentle whisper of the assurance of Jesus, the Jesus who knows us and loves us as we are.

Reflection

Why don't we cry?
What do we believe?
A movie picture leaps from our hearts to our minds.
Jesus, fair-haired, blue-eyed man of grace
Coming to bring joy, prince of peace,
Gentle meek saviour, who we keep in a closed space.

A multi-packaged world stings our eyes,
Rushing to achieve.
Bees at a flower whose nectar is strychnine
The futility of strife.

Colours fade
Bees die
Life ends.
Why don't we cry?
Where is Christ's compassion?
Why are our eyes still dry?
Lord forgive our apathy
Why don't we cry?

Action

Buy a newspaper with a good international section. Use
the stories as a basis for your prayer time.

Prayer

Lord, soften my heart. Enable me to share your passion
for your church and your world.
In Jesus' name,
Amen.

---

[1] See Luke 19: 11-27
[2] See Luke 19: 28-44
[3] See Matthew 15: 32, Matthew 20:34 and Mark 8: 2
[4] See John 11: 1-16
[5] A traditional rhyme taught to children. Source unknown.
[6] See Nehemiah 1:1-3
[7] Nehemiah 1:4-5
[8] Andrew Bonar, *The Life of Robert Murray M'Cheyne*, (Edinburgh: Banner of Truth, 1978) p. 35
[9] Andrew Bonar, *The Life of Robert Murray M'Cheyne*, p. 50
[10] Various, *Bound to be Free*, (Holland: Sovereign International, 1995)

8

Thankfulness

Come and join the celebration

It was three o'clock in the afternoon and we needed to chat. Something had come up in an area of our church life. Whilst it wasn't urgent it would be great if we could get together and talk it through. That was the gist of the message on my phone. I phoned straight back.

'Hi,' I said, 'I am just heading back towards Perth from Aberdeen. We could do coffee later this afternoon if that suits you.'

'That would be great, it's just an idea for outreach that I've been thinking about that I would really like to run by you to see what you think,' he replied. 'Where do you want to meet?'

I tried to think of a place on the outskirts of Perth that would be easy to get parked in front of, a place where we could sit and chat. Remembering a restaurant in a village on the edge of town I suggested we met there in about an hour.

The sun had risen in full glory, surveying the earth below. It was a beautiful spring day and the countryside had a vitality and energy about it. Driving through the countryside, passing farmers in fields and blossoms beginning to burst into colourful anthems of praise, it was a good to be alive. I drove through Cupar Angus, Burrelton and other small villages towards Perth with Louis Armstrong and his Hot Five on the CD player. It was one of these times when you don't want the journey to end, but it was not long before I saw the sign for the restaurant pointing me towards parking on the right.

John stepped out of his car, just as I pulled into a space near the door. He waited for me. We greeted one another, went through the front doors and stepped into a different world.

The first thing that struck us was the din. The noises, indistinguishable at first, like a mass of grenades assaulting the eardrums. After a few seconds it became clear that they were shrieks, cheers, laughter and shouting, all rolled into one. It soon became clear that we had stumbled into a birthday party, with about thirty invited guests – all small children. A few adults sat at a table supervising the mayhem, like censors at a Tarrantino film.

We took a risk and sat at a table in the corner of the room. I had black coffee and John ordered a cappuccino. We started to share what we thought God might be saying to our church and how we could build bridges with the wider community. I have to confess that I was only partly concentrating. Out of the corner of my eye I could see small children diving into a fun pool filled with multi-coloured plastic balls. They were having a great time. There was such joy on those children's faces. They knew how to celebrate. This was fun and they were going to enjoy every last second of it.

About ten minutes later the adults called the children out of the pool. They didn't want to come. They were having too good a time. Eventually they were all rounded up and brought to stand around a large wooden table. Standing at the top of the table was the birthday boy. I heard someone call him Andrew. He was about five years old, with bright orange hair and lots of freckles on his face. His face was red from his exertions in the pool and he displayed the biggest grin that I had ever seen.

Then one of the staff came around the corner carrying a large birthday cake, and all the guests sang with loud and unmelodious voices 'Happy Birthday to you'. Everybody cheered and Andrew laughed with delight. These were his friends and they were sharing in his day, and it was great.

Both John and myself decided that we needed another meeting at a different time and venue. We left the party starting to wind down. Opening the door the spring sun was still there. I got into the car and headed for home. Louis accompanied me again on the CD player with a great solo, playing as only he could.

A few hundred yards along the road I came to a stop sign. Workmen were finishing for the day, leaving a big hole where there should have been road. As I waited, a verse of Scripture came to mind, and I began to picture it in a way I never had before. It is found in the Gospel of Luke, 'I tell you that in the same way there will be more rejoicing in heaven over one sinner who repents than over ninety-nine righteous persons who do not need to repent.' (Lk. 15:6)

All night dancing

'Did you get the box of papers hats?' he asked.

He was strong and very capable, and he looked as if he was in charge. The person that he was speaking to was much younger; he had fair hair and a cheeky grin that gave his face a sort of lopsided look.

'I got them, exactly as you told me to,' he said with a certain air of importance.

The one in charged sighed. 'Well it wouldn't be the first time if you had brought the wrong stuff would it? Your head is always filled with such nonsense, and you're far too nosey for your own good.'

'Well, I got exactly what you told me to get, so you can tick your piece of paper.'

At that, the small messenger dropped the brown box that he had been carrying. It didn't look all that heavy, but he made it seem that carrying it had been a great display of strength. He was the gladiator winning a hard fought contest.

'OK, let's go through the list again,' said the older one rather wearily.

He lifted a bright red clipboard, one that opens up for more paper to be stored. On the front, in gold block capitals, were the words, 'Celebration Checklist Party Poppers'. He gazed at his younger companion who ran to the corner of the room. In the corner there were lots of boxes and bags piled high. Each one had different lettering on the side. He scanned the sides of the boxes then turned back.

'Check,' the younger boy shouted back.

'Whistles?' The boy looked in several bags.

'Check,' he shouted again.

'You don't need to shout. I'm not at the other end of the universe you know,' said the person in charge. As he looked back down to his clipboard, the young one stuck out his tongue and giggled to himself.

'You don't seem to realize how vital this job is – it is a great honour for us to be put in charge of arranging the party. Even though there are millions of them, each one is very special and we have to get it right. Now where was I on the list? Ah, shooting stars and sunbeams.'

* * *

It was another scorching day. There wasn't a breath of breeze. It had been like this all summer. The weather forecaster on television had said it was the hottest summer in the Algarve for ten years.

Luis sat in his taxi waiting for the next tourist wanting to be taken back to their apartment. They usually come all red and exhausted from walking around town, when any local person is resting in the shade. However, it was too hot even for the most determined explorer and things were very quiet. There was only Luis and his taxi. He was proud of his car. It was a cream Mercedes Estate. It was strong, reliable, and trustworthy. It never let him down. 'If only people were as trustworthy, if only people could be relied upon never to let you down.'

As Luis sat in his cab he began to reflect upon the mess in his life. He wondered what had gone wrong. He thought about Anna. He loved her. He had always loved her and would always love her, but if he loved her why had he treated her so badly? They had had rows about money and then his drinking. They used to laugh and dream: now they spat and screamed. Then she told him she couldn't take anymore, slamming the door as she left. Luis knew that she was right. He had let something fragile and beautiful die through his own selfishness. That's when he began to think that almost every chance had been wasted. 'Luis the useless' – that's what they should call me, he thought.

He gazed in his mirror and looked at himself. He looked older than he should for thirty-five years old. His eyes had no sparkle and his hair was starting to grey at the sides. Luis thought about yesterday. He had walked down to the beach at Carvioero, stopped and watched as a young couple laughed and played at the water's edge. It only made him feel more alone. He kicked the sand in frustration, turned and headed back towards his taxi. Just then he had seen a commotion at the corner of the beach shaded by overhanging rocks. He made his way over to see what was happening.

As Luis grew closer he realized that a group of people were singing. There were about thirty people, all of different ages. One or two had guitars, others clapped and sang. Part of him was telling Luis to leave, but his heart wasn't listening. He moved closer to get a better view and to hear what was being said. Before he knew where he was, Luis found himself at the edge of the group.

He watched fascinated as a drama unfolded before him. Luis saw a man stand in the middle of the group. The man spoke and everyone in the group bowed their heads. While he could not fully hear what was being said, Luis realized that the group were praying. Now, like a magnet, he was being pulled towards the group.

Powerpoint – God comes to us in surprising ways. His grace draws us to Jesus.

The whole group moved to the very edge of the water. Then the man who had been leading the prayers stepped into the water and turned back to the group. One of the members of the group came towards the man. Luis wondered what was going to happen. He was in his sixties, with grey hair and a short beard, and he waded out until he reached the leader of the group. Then the leader took him and put him under the water. Luis could not believe his eyes. Was the man being drowned? The leader then lifted the older man back up in the water. They hugged one another. The older man came back to the edge of the beach. Others hugged him.

Then a woman, also about sixty – perhaps the man's wife, waded out into the water. The same thing took place all over again. This happened five more times with three other adults and two teenagers.

The singing began again and the crowd began to drift away. Luis stayed where he was, listening to the music. Something had happened there that had really touched him, but he did not know what. It was then that a young man came over. He was tall and fair. He had on a long pair of blue baggy shorts and a white t-shirt. He smiled at Luis.

'Hi there, how are you?'

'Hi.'

'Did you come to see the baptism?'

The young man moved closer. A baptism, of course thought Luis, angry with himself that he was so slow to recognize what was happening.

'Er no. I heard the singing. I wondered what was happening so I came over to have a look.'

'What did you think of it?' asked the man, a keen interest in his eyes.

'I don't know. It looked strange, funny and important all at the same time.' Luis laughed, 'I thought someone was being drowned at first.'

The young man smiled, 'My name is Jim.' He stretched out his hand. Luis shook it.

'My name is Luis.'

'Luis, we're kinda having a picnic. We've got some food and drink, why don't you come and join us?'

Luis was just about to refuse, to say he had to go back to work. After all he didn't know who these people were. Luis looked at Jim. 'OK,' he said.

He couldn't believe that he had agreed. Yet maybe he just needed some company, someone to chat to. What harm could it do? There was food.

Jim introduced Luis to some of the others. Luis liked them straight away. They were welcoming, but not pushy. They chatted about life and their faith. They believed that God loved them enough to send his son to die for them. They talked about sins forgiven, hope for the hopeless and a new start. A life lived in getting to know Jesus better and following him. Jim explained that he and some of the others were part of a mission team, here for the summer to help a small group of Christians. Luis listened and talked; he told Jim things about his life that he had never told anyone before; the time of darkness, feeling like giving up.

'Well,' said Jim, 'I trust in a God who doesn't give up. Jesus won't give up on you Luis. He died on a cross to save you and if you will only give your life over to him and follow him your life will never be the same again.'

Powerpoint – The good news is that Jesus loved you enough to die for you. Your life can be changed forever.

* * *

'Is it time yet?' The little helper sat, dejected, his head resting upon his hands. 'When is it going to be time? Everything is ready. The balloons, party poppers, hats, flashing stars and sunbeams. I've even got the music ready. Why is it taking so long?'

The person in charge looked at his helper and smiled, 'Have patience, the timing is never in our hands. Do you not think that God knows what he is doing? We will know when the time is right. Until then my little friend we have to wait.'

As Luis continued to ponder the events of the previous day some of Jim's words flashed like neon signposts in his mind.

'Hope for the hopeless.

'God won't give up on you.

'New life.

'He died for you.'

The words went round and round in his head. Jim had given Luis a book, the story of Jesus written by Mark. He had read it through that night. He hadn't been able to put it down. He had heard the story before, but this time it had seemed so very different, so real.

Luis looked again in the mirror of his taxi. This time he saw a man with tears in his eyes. Luis closed his eyes and, after a few moments he spoke.

'Jesus, I believe you died for me
To give me hope, hopeless as I am.
Forgive me and take charge of my life.
Help me. I need your love please.'

The balloons flew through the air. The noise was deafening as the party poppers were let off. Stars shone in their brilliance, a display fit for a king.

And angels danced in celebration.

Rejoice always

The apostle Paul was a man who loved his God and cared passionately about the gospel. Throughout his letters there are wonderful images and illustrations of Paul's walk with the Lord. Philippians is Paul's letter of joy. There is joy in suffering and joy in believing, and in chapter four Paul urges the church to 'Rejoice in the Lord always.' In other words, live in the place of rejoicing.

Joy should be the environment in which we live and breathe. It is the atmosphere in which we grow and move as Christian people. There are two things that come to mind straight away when we consider Paul's letters to the Philippians. First Paul commands the church to rejoice. If he were just thinking about circumstances and life situations it would be a difficult command to keep. However, if joy is not dependent on circumstances, but on the victory of Jesus then it is possible to live in an attitude of joy. Our rejoicing and celebrations are no longer based upon what we wear, where we live or our job prospects, but on our relationship with the living God who, in grace has called us into union with him.

Paul tells the Philippians that this rejoicing should happen continuously. To be in union with Christ is to live in joy. Even when everything appears difficult, and many of the things in which we have relied upon are stripped away, still we can celebrate the great eternal truth found in our relationship with the Saviour.

Powerpoint – To know Jesus is to find lasting joy.

Living the lie

This biblical truth is very hard for us to accept in practice. So much of what the world celebrates is connected to success. To be joyful is to lose thirty pounds and look like a model. An expensive car would also work well – a soft-top sports car would be even better.

In every magazine and every billboard we are being fed a lie. The lie is subtle and effective. It goes like this: true joy can be found in material things. To have is to be happy. Whether it is the perfect shape, the newest house or the right friends, if you want to have joy in your life you've got to get what you can. It is a great shame that we get so easily sucked into this type of thinking. It is hard for us to live as a counter culture, and to be able to say that life doesn't have to be like that. It takes courage to be able to say that who I know is more important than what I have.

> **Powerpoint** – The church can act as a counter culture to the pull of materialism.

As each thing fails to satisfy so we are forced to find another toy or a bigger high to give us what we think we are searching for. This attitude only leads us to become like Verucca Salt in *Willy Wonka and the Chocolate Factory*.[1] As she is shown around the factory, amazing and extraordinary things confront her. Everything she sees she wants. She continually screeches at her father to buy her whatever she wants. The father always has his cheque book at the ready, thinking that buying what she wants will bring happiness to his daughter. This goes on until Willie shows the children and their parents the goose that lays the golden egg.

'I want it and I want it now,' bleats Verucca, but this time she doesn't get what she wants. Rather, through a series of events her greed leads her to being weighed up on a metre, which determines good or bad eggs. She comes up as a bad egg and is rejected. Despite getting nearly everything that she wanted she still wanted more. She has always wanted more, and instead of these material things bringing her joy, all they did was turn her into a bad egg.

As a witness to Jesus we must live in such a way that people can see a difference in us. Could it be that it is God who gives worth and status to people through his love for them? What a wonderful thing it is to know that despite what I have or what I have gone through, I can rejoice because of God's unfaltering love for me. That is a message of wonderful hope in a world of disappointment and shattered dreams.

Do the samba

'I think it was the second on the right, not the left,' I said. 'We've got ten minutes to get there, we don't want to get there late.'

We were travelling in the car to an evening service in a church that we had never visited before. My two friends sat in the front and I sat in the back. All of us had thought that we knew where we were going. The problem was that none of us actually did.

The church that we were visiting met in a school hall. We had been in Atlanta for a course on new church development. Whilst there we had met another student on the course, and it was his church that we were now visiting. He was keen for some Scots to experience it. 'Do you think you will find the way? It's kind of tricky.'

'No problem,' we said with an air of confidence that had proved to be false.

At last, about five minutes before the service started, we stumbled over the venue. There weren't many cars there but it was a new church so we didn't know how many people would be there.

The door was opened and we made our way into the hall. Our friend was waiting and met us with a hug and his usual big bright grin. As we looked around we realized that there were a lot of seats out but very few people sitting on them. In fact there were more people in the praise band than in the congregation. I took a sly look at my watch and found that the service should have started about five minutes before. One of the others in the hall smiled at me:

'Hey it's a Brazilian church, people will turn up when they can, and the worship lasts until it's finished.'

We were told that the service would be mostly in Portuguese and we were given headphones to listen to the translation. However, you don't need a translation for love, fellowship and caring, and we received all of these things.

The band started to play, praising God for all he had done for them. The praise lasted a long time but it felt as if we had hardly begun.

After this time of celebration I looked around and found that the school hall was almost full of people. There were young people and old – young mums with babies in pushchairs and whole families from grandfather through to small grandchildren. The church praised, prayed and listened to the sermon and then praised again. At one point the praise turned into a huge conga dancing around the room as people told one another of the love that God had for them. I hardly understood a word, but I experienced something of the joy of the Lord and the power of praise.

I know that people will point to the culture of those who worshipped and the style of the service. However, what really touched me was the fellowship with some of the congregation after the service finished. Not all those who had been celebrating had successful and prosperous lives. In fact many were living in great times of uncertainty. Yet each one I spoke to talked of the goodness of God, of his faithfulness and mercy in their lives. They were not celebrating because of their circumstances, they were rejoicing in their salvation.

Powerpoint – We can rejoice in God's saving grace in our lives.

Focus on the salvation of God

The story of the Exodus is an epic story of faith and sacrifice, hope and freedom. It is a gripping reminder of the wonderful faithfulness and salvation of God. In Exodus 15 the people have just been released from their captivity in Egypt. God had displayed great power, and now the people were to begin a journey into the unknown. Yet the first thing that the people did was to celebrate the salvation of God: to sing his praises and give thanks for his goodness. Moses and the people sing a song unto the Lord. The theme of the song is found in verse 2:

'The LORD is my strength and my song;
he has become my salvation.
He is my God, and I will praise him,
my father's God, and I will exalt him.'

We are also told that Miriam and the women took tambourines and started to dance in thankfulness for what the Lord had done. The salvation of God had brought a deep sense of faithfulness that in turn had led to an out-pouring of thankfulness and joy.

We see the same thing at the beginning of Luke's Gospel in the song of Mary. An angel of the Lord had told Mary that she was to give birth to a son whom she would call Jesus. He would be called the Son of God. The angel then tells Mary that her relative Elizabeth would also have a child, even though she was in old age.

After the visit Mary sets out to spend some time with Elizabeth. Mary rushes to the town in the hill country where Elizabeth lived. What a journey that must have been. As Mary travelled along the road, I wonder what was going on in her head. How was she going to explain what had happened? What would Elizabeth think about it all? It must have been a journey of huge highs and lows. She would have wanted to celebrate the amazing favour of the Lord, and yet what would others think of her? When Mary arrives she goes into the house and calls out a greeting to Elizabeth and suddenly amazing things happened.

As soon as Elizabeth hears that welcome call the baby in her womb leaps – that must have been a bit of a shock. Then she is suddenly filled with the Holy Spirit and shouts out to Mary, 'Blessed are you among women, and blessed is the child you will bear! But why am I so favoured, that the mother of my Lord should come to me?'

To hear these things from Elizabeth must have been a great strengthening and confirmation for the young woman. This leads to Mary's song of thanksgiving.[2] The song doesn't start with the confirmation, or with any intercessions for Mary or Elizabeth or anybody else. The focus is on the greatness of the Lord. The Lord is the

God of salvation who has poured out his mercy to all those who fear him from generation to generation. While Mary can relate to the wonder of God's grace in her life the thing that becomes her focus is the salvation of the Lord.

While situations may change very rapidly, and circumstances can lift us up or knock us down the salvation of God is constant and sure. Let me ask you a question. Do you spend time reflecting upon the wonder of God's salvation? This really is the foundation of our joy. It is the knowledge that God has saved us for himself, and that we are God's that should make us a people who know how to celebrate. We should be caught in constant delight that God has had mercy upon us. He could have ignored us. He would have been perfectly entitled to turn his back upon us and leave us without any hope. The wonder is that God is not only almighty, but gracious. No longer are we lost, no longer are we strangers, no more are we in darkness. This is all because of the salvation of our God.

Powerpoint – The salvation of God has given us something to be thankful for all our lives.

Imagine what your life would be like now if it had not been for the saving power of God breaking into your life. Just as with tears so with celebration. The people of God are a community who can celebrate together, acknowledging that the situations in which we live alter from moment to moment. Yet we are a thankful people because whatever we face, life will never be the same again. God's salvation has changed everything. Thanks be to God!

Reflection

1. What are the things that bring you joy in life?
2. Paul writes 'Rejoice in the Lord always.' What things fill you most with thanksgiving?
3. Are there things that hinder our attitude of celebration in God's salvation?

Psalm 92

It is good to praise the LORD
and make music to your name, O Most High,
to proclaim your love in the morning
and your faithfulness at night,
to the music of the ten-stringed lyre
and the melody of the harp.
For you make me glad by your deeds O LORD
I sing for joy at the works of your hands.
How great are your works O LORD,
how profound your thoughts! (verses 1-5)

Prayer

God of salvation, help me to fix my mind on the wonder of your grace in my life.
Thank you for loving me, and giving yourself for me.
Thank you that no one can snatch me from your hand.
Thank you that whatever the circumstances of my life you are with me.
Fill me with the joy of your salvation.
In Jesus' lovely name,
Amen

---

[1] Based on the book by Roald Dahl
[2] Luke 1: 46-55

9

Dependence

Let down

As I sat at my desk writing the last section of this book I was listening to the news on the radio. I felt a great sadness at many of the items that I heard. However, one article really made me stop and listen. The story concerned an incident in New Jersey. A couple had been charged with aggravated assault. There is nothing particularly unusual about that you might think. Why would an assault charge end up on the radio in Scotland? The reason was that the assault was against their children. The couple had four adopted sons who were found to be severely malnourished. The reporter went on to explain that the boys were so emaciated that it was impossible to tell their ages. Police were alerted when neighbours saw the oldest as he raked through rubbish bins desperately hunting for something to eat. The correspondent concluded the report by stating that the oldest son weighed only nineteen kilograms when he was found.

I sat stunned for a minute trying to work out what nineteen kilograms was in stones, pounds and ounces. It must be about three stone. I tried to work it out again as I could not believe that a nineteen-year-old boy could weigh so little. Yet I seemed to get my sums almost correct: just over three stone.

I went over, switched off the radio and went back to my desk. I sat reflecting for a few minutes before asking God to be with these children. As I thought about the situation of these children and many others I realized that a vital thing for children is to have someone that they can depend upon. There must be someone that loves the child enough to give them a sense of belonging and safety. It is in this type of atmosphere that children can grow and develop. They can celebrate, grow, laugh and cry if they know that someone will always be there for them. Without that safety net, some of the childlike qualities will be stunted.

Waiting for dad

I was about to get back to work when I looked up at a print that I have on my study wall. It is a copy of a watercolour by the American artist Winslow Homer, painted in 1875. It is a seaside scene. The beach is a mix of light and dark sand with pebbles sprinkled over the surface. The sea is calm and is a light blue colour with hardly a splash of white to indicate a wave. On the horizon there are several sailing ships that must have been moving very slowly in the settled conditions.

The only character in the picture is a young boy. He is sitting on a small rowing boat, which is moored on the beach. He is dressed in blue jeans and a dark brown shirt. On his head is a neat little white hat with a blue band. Anything could have been happening on the beach behind the boy as he is clearly concentrating on other things. He gazes longing out to sea, obviously waiting on his father coming back from a voyage.

While there is no picture of the father I think of the time when the young boy's dad would step on to the shore and be greeted by his son running along the pebbled beach. I imagine the dad reaching down to lift the boy who had been waiting for him. It is the longing of the child for his father that makes the picture so captivating.

This is what we need if our lives are going to be marked by our closeness to the Lord. In an age where so many of us have experienced letdown, it is difficult for us to give ourselves unreservedly to anyone. While we may give mental assent to the fact that God can be trusted, it can still be hard to be open up in our spiritual lives; to allow God into the areas of bruising in our lives and to let him bring healing.

Just as important is the knowledge that we can depend upon the God who will never fail us. If we accept that God can be trusted then we can step out into new things and head in new directions. If God is really never going to let us down then there are no obstacles that we cannot tackle and overcome. As children we find our peace and direction only when we come to know that God is utterly dependable.

Just take over

It is always difficult to take over from someone who has done a great job. Natural leaders are not easy to find and when one does comes to an end of their ministry they are hard to replace. Try and think of someone who has been a risk taker, somebody who has really pushed an area of life in a new direction. When they stopped, who replaced them? The shadow of a powerful person is a long one, and it is difficult to get from under it.

Joshua chapter one begins with the words, 'After the death of Moses the servant of the LORD.' Wow, what a comment. Moses, the person called by God to lead the people out of slavery in Egypt. This is the man who was called a 'friend of God.'[1] He was a leader who kept going despite countless difficulties and disappointments. Many times the people let him down and brought him almost to the point of despair, but he knew that he could depend upon God. After all was it not God who had called him and sustained him from the very beginning? While other people may have let Moses down and others had moaned and complained, still God was with him.

Now Moses had died without managing to take the people into the land that was flowing with milk and honey, the land of Canaan. Instead God calls Joshua to take over the role of leader.

To be leader of this people could really have been a poison chalice. Not only did he have the weight of following Moses, but also the expectations of taking the people into a place that they had never been able to go to before. For any person this would have been a monumental task but Joshua had been Moses' assistant. Joshua had seen the pressures close-up, and he would have known more than any other about the gifts that

Moses had, and the problems that he had faced. To be called to lead must have been a huge responsibility and great honour.

Powerpoint – Whatever challenges God gives you, he will give you the grace to do it.

All of this may have caused most of us to panic but Joshua had something wonderful to hold onto. Joshua had the promise of God. He was reminded at the start of his leadership that the Lord would be with him. Joshua was going to be able to face new things and overcome opposition because he knew that he would be able to depend on God. Just listen to the promises that Joshua was given as he took up his new post:

'I will give you every place where you set your foot.' (verse 3)
'As I was with Moses, so I will be with you. I will never leave you nor forsake you' (verse 5)
'Have I not commanded you? Be strong and courageous. Do not be terrified; do not be discouraged, for the LORD your God will be with you wherever you go.' (verse 9)

God is saying to Joshua. 'You will be able to do whatever it is that I ask you to do because the Lord your God will be you. It will not be down to your leadership, or to the people. It will be because I am with you.'

This is the key for all who seek to grow in closeness to God. Everything we have discussed in this book points to the fact that the Lord is with us. He has a plan for your life, and as you learn to open up to God then you will find that God never fails. He has promised that he will never leave you nor will he forsake you. So now is the opportunity to deepen your spiritual life and begin to prepare for all eternity with the one who will be with you always. As Christians there is nothing that we cannot achieve for God if we spend our lives dependent upon him.

Powerpoint – Dream big dreams – God is able.

Someone to lean on

Literature is full of people who can only progress to do great things because they know that they have someone in whom they can trust. Think of Sherlock Holmes and his various adventures. With a razor-sharp intellect he works out cases that no one else can solve. He dissects information and sorts through clues; there are even times when he goes in disguise to track down some missing piece required to make sense of the case. Yet throughout all these adventures there is always Dr Watson. It is Dr Watson who is always steady and reliable. Whether it is to listen or to offer vital back-up, he is always trustworthy. He is someone on whom Holmes can rely. Again and again when Holmes is half way through a case and is in the depth of despair, it is Dr Watson's word of encouragement, or sometimes simply his presence that keeps him going.

Another hero who could not have gone forward without the help of someone else is Frodo in the *The Lord of the Rings*. I read the books twice when I was younger but was absolutely captivated by the film version. The scene that sticks in my memory is at the end of the first film, *The Fellowship of the Ring*. Frodo is standing looking out into a lake. He is gazing at the other side deciding what he should do and whether he has the courage to go on.

After hearing the voice of Gandalf, Frodo gets into a rowing boat and heads for the unknown. Just as he starts rowing his friend Sam Gangee comes running out of the trees and onto the beach shouting out for Frodo. Frodo continues to row and shouts back to Sam telling him to stay. Sam plunges into the water trying to catch up with the boat. Frodo urges him to go back. Then there is a wonderful line. Frodo calls back, 'I am going on myself Sam.'

'Of course you are,' shouts back Sam, 'and I'm going with you.'

Sam almost drowns and Frodo has to turn back and pick him up. When they are both in the boat they turn to one another and Sam states, 'I made a promise not to leave Mr Frodo and I don't need to.' The last scene shows the two of them on top of a mountain looking into another land. They are unsure what awaits them or what happened to the rest of their friends. What they know is that things will be tough for them. Frodo looks at Sam and says quietly, 'Sam I am glad you are with me.'

Jesus made some wonderful promises. Think of the following statements:

'My sheep listen to my voice; I know them and they follow me. I give them eternal life, and they shall never perish, no-one shall snatch them from my hand.' (Jn. 10:27)

'Come to me all you who are weary and burdened, and I will give you rest.' (Mt. 11:28)

'And surely I am with you always, to the very end of the age.' (Mt. 28:20)

We could go on and on looking at the promises that Jesus made but ultimately the point is a simple one – Jesus is the one that we can trust. We are called to base our lives

and our walk with God not on ourselves, or on any circumstances that we face, but on the fact that Jesus has
promised to be with us. We can grow in our spiritual
lives secure in the knowledge that we are held in the very
hands of almighty God. There can never be a safer place
for us to rest than in the hands of God. That is where we
find our assurance.

As children of God we can let go of the things that
hinder us, knowing that God is not going to let go of us.
He is with us. This is the most vital thing for us to
remember that while we are called to deepen and grow
in our relationship with God, we can only do this
because of God's great grace and goodness towards us.
This should be our encouragement: that God enjoys
being in fellowship with us and calls us to an ever more
loving and intimate union with him.

Reflection

I am trusting Thee, Lord Jesus,
Trusting only Thee;
Trusting Thee for full salvation,
Great and free.

I am trusting Thee for pardon;
At Thy feet I bow;
For Thy grace and tender mercy,
Trusting now.

I am trusting thee to guide me;
Thou alone shalt lead,
Every day and hour supplying
All my need.

(Frances Ridley Havergal)[2]

Action

Think carefully about every area of your life. Write
down the things that you feel you should hand over to
God. Pray, asking God to deal with each one. Then rip
up the piece of paper and put the pieces into bin.
Thank God that we can trust him with the whole of
our lives.

Prayer

Thank you Lord that you are completely trustworthy.
I praise you Lord that you will never leave, and that you

will guide and strengthen me throughout my life with
you.
Amen.

---

[1] Exodus 33: 11
[2] Verses 1, 2 and 4 only

Conclusion

The windscreen wipers had been working overtime ever since we left the house. Early that morning we had packed the car and set off from Perth. Our destination was the Isle of Skye. Our schedule had been very busy and we needed a break for a few days.

The Isle of Skye is a great place for the family. You have no choice but to slow down and unwind. We had decided to stay at a lovely retreat house at the north end of the island. We had been to Skye before and we knew that the people were wonderfully welcoming. It is always good to be surrounded by the warmth of a Highland welcome. The type that Rabbie Burns reflects upon in his poem, 'A Highland Welcome'.[1]

It's a long drive to Skye, and with two young children in the back of the car we needed plenty of distractions. We had played at counting cars, telling stories and drawing pictures. All of these things helped keep the boredom at bay making the trip more manageable. After a while we put on a tape of *George's Marvellous Medicine* by Roald Dahl. We all laughed at his quirky view of the world. Meanwhile, the rain continued to hurl itself at the car. It was so heavy that even the beautiful scenery was lost to us.

Eventually the boys fell asleep. Caroline put a James Taylor CD on and we sang along to his relaxing style,

'Don't you know that you've got a friend?' We had been driving for over three hours and the rain had stopped at last. We decided that we would stop for a coffee before we headed across the Skye Bridge. We drove down towards the Kyle of Lochalsh. As the road wound down towards the town a small sleepy voice was heard.

'Mummy, mummy I spy a rainbow.'

Our son was right, there in the sky was God's multi-coloured declaration of hope. There had been so many things to consider, so much to think about that we almost missed what became a moment of great joy. It was a glimpse of grace that brightened up the whole day. It took a child to see it and become excited by it. It was a child who saw what was really important.

I began this book by reminding us all of how wonderful it is to be loved by God. My prayer is that as you have journeyed through this book, you will have found a deeper joy in your ongoing relationship with God. Despite the clouds, rain and mist that may descend upon your life, I pray that you may find a childlike glee in spying the rainbow: living the kingdom life in an evermore intimate walk with the Lord.

---

[1] Robert Burns, *The Complete Work of Robert Burns*, ed. James A. MacKay (Ayrshire: Alloway Publications, 1990)

Bibliography

Books

Bonar, A., *The Life of Robert Murray M'Cheyne* (Edinburgh: Banner of Truth, 1978. Second reprint).

Burns, R., *The Complete Works of Robert Burns*, ed. James A. MacKay (Ayrshire: Alloway Publications, 1990)

Carson, D., *The Gospel According to John* (Downers Grove: IVP, 1991)

Dahl R., *Charlie and the Chocolate Factory* (London: Penguin, 2001)

Dahl R., *George's Marvellous Medicine* (London: Penguin, 1997)

Kidner, D., *Genesis* (Leicester: IVP, 1967)

Newbigin, L., *Proper Confidence* (Grand Rapids: Eerdmans, 1995)

Parks, R., *Quiet Strength* (Grand Rapids: Zondervan, 1994)

Peterson, E., *The Message* (Colorado Springs: Navpress, 1993)

Stott, J., *Message of Acts* (Leicester: IVP, 1990)

Tolkien, J.R.R., *The Lord of the Rings* (London: Harper Collins, 1991)

Washington, James Melvin (ed), *I Have a Dream: Writings and Speeches that Changed the World* (London: Harper Collins, 1992)

Williams, David J., *Acts* (Carlisle: Paternoster Press, 1995)

Various, *Bound to be Free* (Holland: Sovereign International, 1995)

Films

Casablanca, VHS. Directed by Michael Curtiz. (1942; Warner Home Video, 2000)

Pete's Dragon, VHS. Directed by Don Chaffey. (1977; Disney, 2000)

Raiders of the Lost Ark, VHS. Directed by Steven Spielberg. (1981; Paramount Home Entertainment, 2000)

The Lord of the Rings, VHS. Directed by Peter Jackson. (2001; New Line Cinema, 2002)

The Wizard of Oz, VHS. Directed by Victor Fleming. (1939; MGM,1997)